The techniques and projects in this chapter are all very quick and easy to do – almost instant, in fact. Read the steps through carefully before you begin and assemble all the materials you will need. Once you are prepared, you will be astonished at how quickly you can work.

in an instant

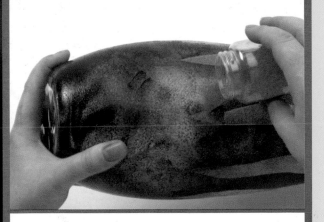

outlining

Vinyl outlines

These vinyl motifs are definitely the simplest and fastest way of creating an outline. There are thousands of designs available in a range of colours; you just peel, stick and paint. They can be applied directly onto glass or stuck onto glass painting film, which can then be painted, cut out and stuck onto glass.

You can also just stick vinyl outlines onto pre-painted glass to add decoration. They even work well on light bulbs up to 40 watts, but you must use a light bulb paint to paint the bulbs.

MATERIALS
Vinyl outline
Self-adhesive glass
   painting film
Water-based glass paints
Paintbrush
Scissors
Glass

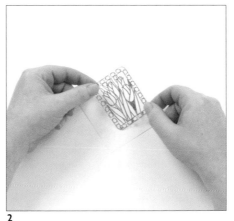

1

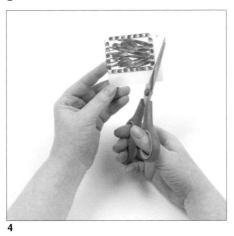

2

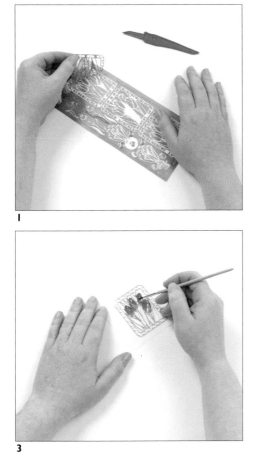

3

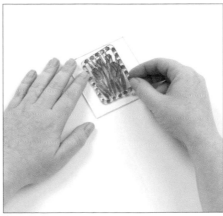

4

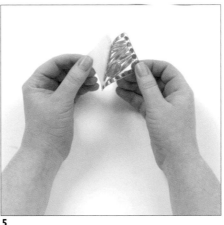

5

6

TAKING IT FURTHER

You don't have to paint the whole design; leave some areas blank to take on the colour of their background, in this case white for snow.

A black outline and strong colours create a clean, graphic design.

1 It is easy to just peel the designs off the backing sheet, though you may find a craft knife useful for lifting the first corner.

2 Stick the outline onto a piece of self-adhesive glass painting film, or straight onto a piece of glass. Just position the design and press it down flat.

3 Paint the design with either solvent-based paints or slightly thinned water-based paints. Because the vinyls don't have a raised, defined outline, let each section dry before painting the adjacent section, so that the paints do not flow into each other.

4 If you have worked on self-adhesive film, when the paint is dry, cut around the outline with sharp scissors.

5 Peel away the backing sheet.

6 Stick the film onto the glass carefully, ensuring that there are no air bubbles underneath. You can stick these painted motifs onto any glass surface — a window or mirror for example.

Stamping an outline

There are so many rubber stamps on the market and they offer another easy way of creating an outline. You can stamp the design in black and then paint it, as for the vinyl outlines, or you can stamp using water-based paints to create a coloured outline – an instant, painted design. You can also stamp onto pre-painted glass to add decoration.

MATERIALS
Stamp
Water-based glass paints
Paintbrush
Glass

1 Brush water-based paint onto the rubber face of the stamp. For this rose stamp we brushed red onto the flower and green onto the leaves. Take care not to over-paint the stamp, or the paint will spread when stamped onto the glass.
2 Carefully place the stamp onto the glass and press down gently.
3 Cleanly and swiftly lift the stamp off the glass to reveal the red rose and green leaves.

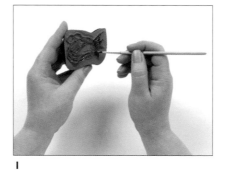

1

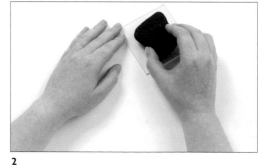

2

3

SUCCESSFUL STAMPING

If the paint smudges a little it is best to let it dry and then tidy it up with a craft knife. Clean your stamp with a damp cloth and then dry it off after use, or the moisture may cause the rubber to perish.

TAKING IT FURTHER

This piece of glass was rubber stamped and then painted. Once the colours were dry, a thin layer of clear water-based glass paint was fingerpainted over the surface to age it a little.

A background was created on this piece of glass by painting it and then piping gold outliner onto the wet paint. Once the background was dry, a design was stamped onto it using a foam stamp and black ink.

A smooth, fingerpainted glass surface is an ideal background for this delicate floral stamp.

Outliner in sheets

If spread out thinly outliner, when dry, forms a skin that can be cut into strips and used to make designs, which can be painted in the usual way. This is a good technique for making simple designs. You can also cut shapes out of the outliner and stick them onto coloured or painted glass.

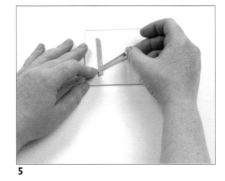

MATERIALS
Release paper
Outliner
Scissors
Glass

1 Squeeze some outliner onto a sheet of release paper.

2 Brush or fingerpaint the outliner over the release paper using a side-to-side motion. Leave it to dry overnight

3 When the outliner is dry it will peel off like a skin. You can either peel it off and save the release paper to use again, or cut the outliner out on the paper.

4 You can cut out the outliner with scissors; we have just cut it into simple strips.

5 Lay the pieces of outliner onto the glass and they will cling to the surface.

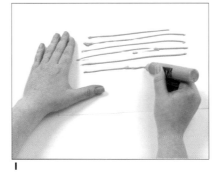

1

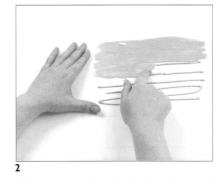

2

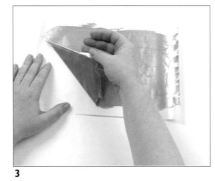

3

4

5

TAKING IT FURTHER

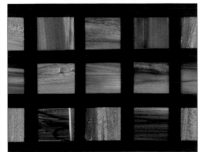

Fingerpainted mosaic (see page 55) can be delineated with thin strips of black outliner.

Here a flower design was cut out of a sheet of silver outliner and put onto a pre-painted glass square.

Outliner on self-adhesive film

You can finger paint or brush outliner in any colour onto self-adhesive film. When it is dry you can cut it into strips, peel the backing sheet away and stick to the glass to act as an outline. This technique is good for creating straight lines. If you cut the outliner with decorative-edge scissors, the resulting strips make good borders.

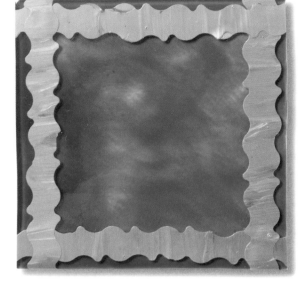

MATERIALS
Self-adhesive glass
    painting film
Outliner
Decorative-edge
    scissors
Coloured glass

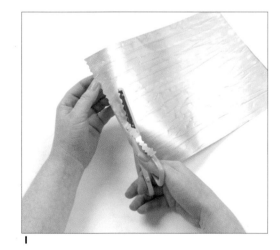

1

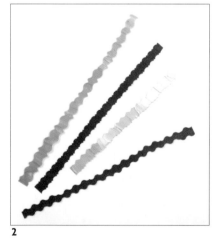

2

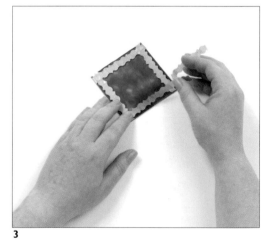

3

1 Fingerpaint the outliner onto the film and leave it to dry (see page 13). Using decorative-edge scissors, cut a strip of the film.
2 Assorted strips of film cut with different decorative-edge scissors.
3 Peel off the backing and stick the strip onto coloured or painted glass.

TAKING IT FURTHER

You can also draw shapes onto the back of the film, cut them out, peel away the backing sheet and stick them onto glass.

Stamping mosaic

Stamping a mosaic pattern with a foam sponge from the bathroom is so easy. Cut the squares of foam carefully, so that they are all the same size, and then just stamp away.

MATERIALS
Foam sponge
Scissors
Plate
Water-based glass
  paints
Glass

1 Using scissors, cut the sponge into strips about 2cm (¾in) thick and then cut these strips into squares.

2 Squeeze your chosen paint colours onto a plate and dip your sponges into them, using a separate sponge for each different colour. Then just stamp the mosaic design onto the glass.

TAKING IT FURTHER
The same simple technique can be used on a shaped glass item, such as a vase.

MAKING A PALETTE
Cover the plate with plastic food wrap and squeeze the paint onto this. When you have finished, just throw the food wrap away.

1

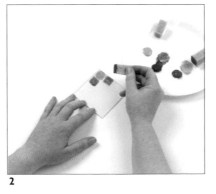

2

CLEANING SPONGES
You can use the sponges time and time again, if you wash them out every time you use them. Be sure to wash them before the paint has chance to dry.

painting

Masking and sponging

There are many ways to mask off glass for painting – you can use masking tape, masking fluid or sticky-backed plastic. However, one of the most versatile ways is to cut a design out of paper and stick it to the glass with spray glue. Sponging works well with masking, as does stippling. It is usually best to peel the paper off the glass before the paint is dry, as if you remove it when the paint has fully dried you run the risk of pulling some of the paint away as well. However, do test this with the brand of paint that you are using.

MATERIALS
Paper
Scissors
Spray glue
Plate
Water-based glass
  paints
Sponge
Craft knife

1 Photocopy a design onto plain paper and cut the design out. Lightly spray one side with glue.
2 Stick the paper onto the glass.
3 Squeeze some paint onto a plate and dip the sponge into it. Sponge paint over the whole surface of the glass, sponging over the edges of the paper. Do not put too much paint onto the sponge or it may creep under the edges of the paper.
4 While the paint is still wet, use a craft knife to lift one corner of the paper. Be very careful not to smudge the paint.
5 Peel off the paper mask to reveal the design.

1

2

3

4

5

TAKING IT FURTHER
Simple shapes work best with this technique. If you use a complicated paper design you are more likely to smudge the paint when you peel the paper off the glass. You can use more than one colour of paint and blend them together as you sponge them on.

Stamping around a mask

You can buy many different foam shapes – try a toy shop for some fun, small ones or you can cut out your own. Just draw your design onto the sponge with a felt-tip pen and cut it out with scissors. You can stick the shape to the back of a piece of high-density foam a little bigger then the design itself to make it easier to stamp with.

MATERIALS
Foam stamp
Water-based glass
  paints
Plate
Glass
Paper
Scissors
Foam sponge
Craft knife

1 Stamp the shape onto the glass and onto a piece of paper.
2 When the paint is dry, cut the shape out of the paper.
3 Place the paper shape over the stamped one on the glass to act as a mask. Stamp the square as described in Stamping Mosaic (see page 15).
4 When you have finished the stamping, lift off the paper mask to reveal the untouched design beneath. A craft knife is useful for lifting a corner of the paper so that you can lift the rest off cleanly.

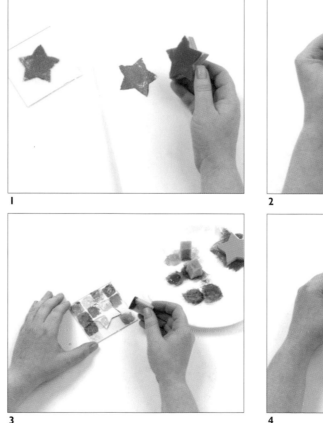

1

2

3

4

Fingerpainting onto photocopy film

This must be one of the quickest and easiest ways to create a coloured design. The self-adhesive film is designed to go through a photocopier, so any design or text can be printed onto it. Then you just fingerpaint the design, cut it out and stick to glass. It is best to use water-based paints, as solvent-based ones will smudge the photocopy.

MATERIALS
Self-adhesive
  photocopy film
Water-based glass
  paints
Sharp scissors

MOVING THE DESIGN

If you wish to re-position the design on the glass, just peel it off and re-apply it, keeping your fingers away from the sticky side of the film. The longer the film is on the glass, the harder it will be to remove. You can immerse the glass in hot water and leave it to soak for a short while to soften the glue and allow you to peel off the design. When dry, the design can be stored on a piece of release paper and used again. Alternatively, use a hot hair dryer to help soften the glue. Glass decorated with film can be hand-washed and dried, but do not soak it or put it in a dishwasher.

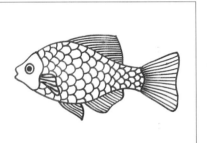

1

2

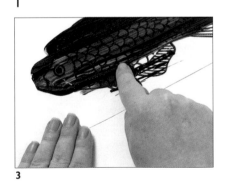

3

4

5

1 Photocopy a design onto the self-adhesive photocopy film. If necessary, enlarge the design onto plain paper first and then copy it onto the film.
2 Streak the paint straight from the bottle right across the photocopied design. Keep the streaks quite thin and vary the colours as you wish.
3 Use your index finger to gently smooth the paint over the design, using a side-to-side motion. The colours will blend naturally. Do not be tempted to swirl the

colours together, the end result will just be messy.
4 Before the paint dries, with the tip of a clean finger or a brush, wipe some of the paint out of the fish's eye and squeeze a blob of the clear paint onto it. Leave the fish to dry.
5 Cut out the design with sharp scissors. Peel off the backing sheet to reveal the sticky side and stick the design to the glass, smoothing out any bubbles as you go.

Printing with leaves

In spring and summer printing with leaves is easy, but winter can bring problems – no leaves. However, don't despair, you can use the leaves from silk flowers and plants. Even house plants can be used, but be careful as the sap in the leaves of some plants can be toxic.

MATERIALS
Leaf
Water-based glass
  paints
Paintbrush
Glass
Kitchen towel

1

TAKING IT FURTHER

The leaves from silk flowers and plants can be used to make excellent prints.

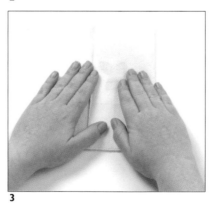

3

4

1 Take your chosen leaf, ensuring that it is clean and free of insects. Place it on a piece of paper and with a flat-headed brush, paint your chosen colours thinly over the leaf.

2 Place the glass on a piece of kitchen towel. Carefully lay the leaf paint-side down onto the glass.

3 Fold the kitchen towel over the leaf and gently press down. Lift off the paper towel – it should pick up any of the paint that has seeped out from beneath the leaf.

4 Then carefully peel off the leaf.

This square of glass was painted and then printed with a silk leaf and silver outliner, brushed on in the same way as paint.

Stencilling

You can make stencilling as simple and quick or as intricate and time-consuming as you like. There are thousands of pre-cut designs on the market, or you can cut your own designs out with the help of a craft knife or a hot stencil cutter.

When stencilling, hold the stencil firmly so that it does not move. You may wish to tape it down with low-tack masking tape or use spray glue on the back of the stencil to keep it in position.

MATERIALS
Stencil
Water-based glass
  paints
Stencil brush
Plate
Coloured glass

1 Lay the stencil over the glass and simply stipple on the paint thinly with a stencil brush. Do not try to apply the paint thickly or it may bleed underneath the stencil.

2 Carefully peel the stencil away from the glass to reveal the design. Immediately wipe any excess paint off the stencil.

SUCCESSFUL STENCILLING

When stencilling onto pre-painted glass, always make sure that the paint has dried thoroughly before you start. If it is not dry, you may pull the paint off the glass as you peel away the stencil.

If paint should spread we find it best to let it dry and then just cut away the excess paint with a craft knife.

For intricate stencils you can use a cotton bud to apply the paint to the smallest areas of the design.

Keep yogurt pot, margarine and ice cream lids to cut stencils from. Draw the design and cut it out with a craft knife. The raised edges of the lids are useful to hold on to as you stencil.

TAKING IT FURTHER

Make your own quick, easy and disposable stencils with a paper punch.

Punch holes in a piece of medium-weight paper or thin card.

Apply paint through the punched holes with a small sponge. When you have finished, just throw the paper away.

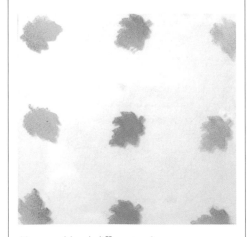

You can blend different colours as you sponge for a more interesting finish. Small stencils work well for adding detail to glass-painted projects.

1

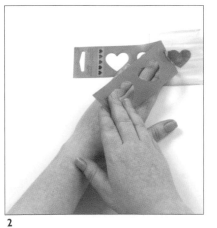

2

Hand-printing

Children, like Matthew who made these prints for us, love this technique. We once made a hand-print collage for a front door, using the hands of every member of the family and even the paws of the pet dog. It was very colourful and unusual and was a good talking point. We signed the work for fun with a fingerprint in the corner. You must use a water-based paint for this technique. If you are worried about an allergic reaction or have a skin condition, you can use a tight rubber glove, but you will lose the fine lines on your skin.

MATERIALS
Acetate
Water-based glass
  paints
Paintbrush
Hands

1 Squeeze some paint onto a sheet of plastic and brush it out.
2 Then just place your hand in the paint and gently press down.
3 Then press your hand onto the glass and lift off carefully, leaving your hand print on the glass. Repeat in as many colours as you wish. If you don't want the paints to smudge into each other, dry each colour with a hair dryer before printing the next one.

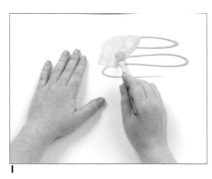

1

2

3

CHILD SAFETY
If you are working with children, try getting them to print onto a sheet of acetate that can then be stuck into a window, it's safer and easier for them to do.

TAKING IT FURTHER

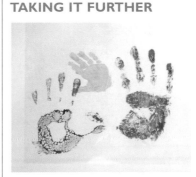

A print picture made by the whole family; you can also include a pet's paw print, but do be sure to wash the animal's foot afterwards.

This is an interesting variation on this technique – a fingerpainted mosaic vase. Work in two colours, with one finger for each, and try not to dip the wrong finger in the wrong paint.

Marbling

This is one of those techniques that takes no time to do, but can look really effective. It gives a marbled effect and you can change the paint colours to make any colour of marble you want. We made ours in amber, gold and white water-based paint.

MATERIALS
Water-based glass
   paints
Outliner
Paintbrush
Glass
Plastic food wrap

1

2

3

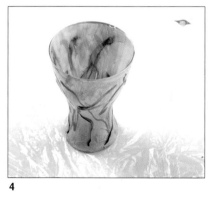

4

5

6

7

1 Squeeze the white paint onto the glass and fingerpaint it to cover the whole vase.

2 Squeeze some gold paint onto the white paint and roughly blend it in with the tips of your fingers.

3 Next, load your brush with some amber paint and just streak it randomly onto the vase, like the veins in marble.

4 Tear off two lengths of plastic food wrap, enough to cover the vase completely. Lay them flat on the work surface in a cross shape and stand the vase in the middle.

5 Take the corners of the plastic wrap and bring them up and over the vase to completely cover all of the glass.

6 This is the best bit; just squidge the paint under the film so that it blends a little, but don't overdo it or it will blend too much and you will just have a brown vase.

7 Peel the wrap off the vase to reveal the marbled effect. If there is an area that you are not happy with, replace the section of film and squidge it again.

Crackle effect

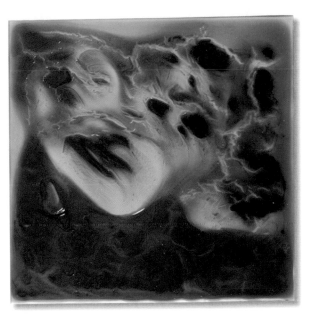

You can buy some spray cans that give a great crackled effect, but you can also create crackle with water-based glass paints. However, this only works on flat glass or film, as you have to water down the paint to make it flow. The resulting finish works very well on squares in mosaic projects (see Textured Mosaic Panel, page 70).

MATERIALS
Water-based glass paints
  in two colours
Water
Brush
Glass
Hairdryer

I Water down the paints so they flow well (about one part water to one part paint) and paint the glass with them, mixing the colours as you work. Then take some clear water and drip it randomly on the paint.
2 While the paint is wet, dry it quickly with a hair dryer. The paint will get a skin on the top and start to dry. As the paint below the surface layer dries, it will crack and depending on the angle of the blast from the hair dryer, you can push the paint around, creating thick and thin areas of paint.

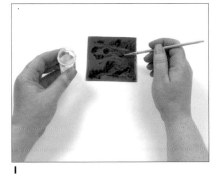

I

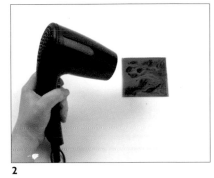

2

TAKING IT FURTHER

Store-bought crackle paints have two coats, an undercoat and a topcoat, which crackles in a matter of minutes. Check the manufacturer's instructions on which surfaces you can use it on and how to do it. Make sure that you always read the safety instructions as well.

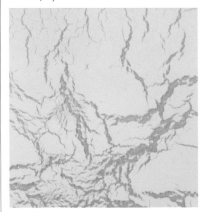

A gold undercoat with a cream crackled topcoat.

A brown undercoat with a burgundy crackled topcoat.

Painting texture

You don't have to use a brush when you are glass painting. Look around you – that plastic shopping bag, the bubble wrap from around the glass vase you bought, some screwed-up paper, tissue, fabric or even lace can be used to paint and create texture with. Squeeze the paint onto a plate and dip your chosen applicator into it, then press it onto the glass for simple, fantastic results.

MATERIALS
Bubble wrap or plastic
  bag
Plate
Water-based paints
Glass

1 Take a small piece of bubble wrap and fold it neatly so that the bubbles are not scrunched up. Dip this into the paint.

2 Gently dab the bubble wrap onto the glass. Do not dab twice in the same place or you may lose the textured effect.

3 If you are going to add another layer of colour, use a clean piece of bubble wrap to help keep the colours defined.

4 The same technique can be used with a screwed-up plastic bag to create a different texture.

5 Apply the paint to the glass with the plastic bag. You can alter the effect by how loosely or tightly you screw up the bag.

1

2

3

CHOOSING PAINT

These techniques work best using undiluted water-based paint applied in a thin layer to give you good colour coverage.

Dry each layer of coloured paint with a hairdryer if you wish – this helps to keep the colours defined.

4

5

Attaching glass decorations

A quick way to transform any glass is to stick some glass shapes onto it using silicone glue. The glue is tacky enough to hold light-weight shapes in place while it dries, but for heavier shapes it is best to use a piece of masking tape to hold them in place until the glue has dried.

MATERIALS
Glass shapes
Silicone glue
Glass

1 Apply a blob of glue to the back of the glass shape.
2 Then simply stick it down onto the glass.

1

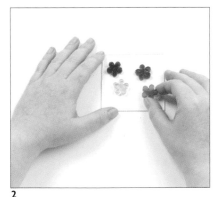

2

TAKING IT FURTHER

There is a wide range of glass shapes available and they provide a very quick way of cheering up a vase or mirror, though the item must be hand-washed carefully and shouldn't come into contact with food.

Using coloured sand

You can decorate painted glass by using double-sided sticky tape and sand. Double-sided tape is available on a reel in various thicknesses and can also be bought in sheet form.

Decorative sand comes in various colours and grain sizes, but you can also use fine glass beads or glitter. In fact, you can use any product with a fine texture. You can seal the sand with a coat of spray varnish, though this isn't necessary unless you are going to handle the item a lot.

The glass doesn't have to be painted – you can use this technique on plain glass as well.

MATERIALS
Double-sided sticky
  tape or sheet
Glass
Coloured sands

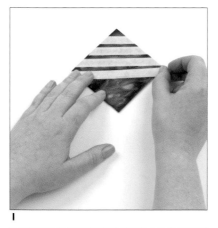

1

2

3

4

5

1 Cut lengths of double-sided tape to fit the piece of glass; if they are a little long they can be trimmed once stuck down. Peel away one backing sheet and stick the tape to the glass. Press it down so that it sticks firmly.

2 Peel away the other backing sheet to reveal the sticky tape, taking care not to get your fingers on it, as this may affect it's stickiness.

If you are using only one colour of sand, peel all the backings away. If

SUCCESSFUL SANDING

Always keep coloured sands in a warm, dry place or the sand with stick together and not flow freely. To clean an item decorated with sand, just wipe it carefully with a damp, lint-free cloth – never submerge the item in water or the sticky tape will come loose and all your decoration will just float off the glass. If the item will be frequently handled, a coat of spray varnish will protect it and will help keep the sand attached to the tape.

1

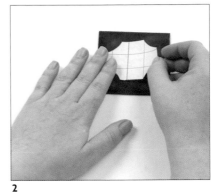

2

3

1 The same technique is used with double-sided sticky sheet, but you can cut it into shapes. Peel one backing sheet off the cut-out shape.

2 Stick the shape onto a painted piece of glass and press it down firmly, then peel off the other backing sheet.

3 Sprinkle sand onto the sticky shape. You can use different colours, sprinkling them in areas to create a graduated effect. Press the sand down with your fingers, then tip away the excess. The excess sand is a mix of different colours, so you can to throw it away or store it in its own jar to use later.

you are using various colours, only peel away the area you want to cover with a particular colour.

3 Sprinkle the sand onto the tape. If you decant some sand into a piece of folded paper it is easy to control the amount you sprinkle on.

4 Pat the sand gently but firmly with your finger to help stick it to the tape.

5 Tip the excess sand onto a piece of paper and return it to the jar, then continue with the next colour of sand.

Texture from patterned surfaces

You can apply water-based paint to many textured surfaces, though it works best on flat surfaces: glass, ceramic, metal and plastic are just a few materials that you can work on. When the paint is dry, it can be peeled off and the texture of the surface will be embedded into it. If you choose a patterned plastic, you will need to brush a thin layer of grease onto it, getting into all the nooks and crannies with the brush. This will stop the paint sticking to the plastic and make it easy to peel off.

You can even incorporate other substances into the layers of paint as they dry – beads, sand, gold leaf, fabric, etc.

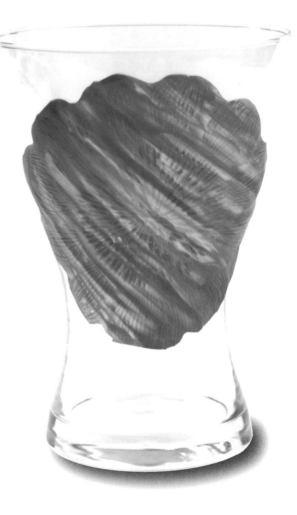

MATERIALS
Patterned glass
Water-based glass
  paints
Scissors
Glass

1 Squeeze the paints directly from the bottle onto the patterned glass. The glass we have chosen is a plate with a raised flower design.

2 Then just finger paint from side-to-side lightly over the area of the glass you want to use. Leave it to dry.

3 To make the layer of paint thicker, so that it peels away easily without splitting, apply a couple of layers of clear paint. You can apply more layers of colour, but the tones will become very dense. Leave it to dry, preferably overnight.

4 When it is all dry, just peel the paint away from the glass. You may find it easier to use a craft knife to lift the corner, and then peel the paint off with your fingers.

1

2

3

4

5 Where the paint has gone over the edges of the design, just cut off the excess with a pair of scissors.

6 The design will cling to any smooth surface. If you want it to stick more permanently, coat the back with spray glue and then stick it on to the surface.

5

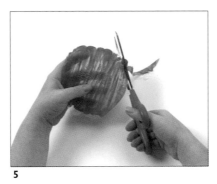

6

A PAINTED FLOWER

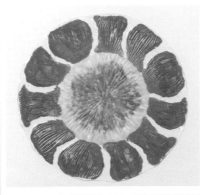

If you prefer you can use a brush to paint the glass first, highlighting the design, and then fingerpaint a layer of clear paint over the colours once they are dry. This will give you a more defined design.

SUCCESSFUL TEXTURE

Make sure your pattered surface is clean and dry before you work on it. A gentle wash in light soapy water is enough.

When the paint is wet it will be opaque, but as it dries it will become more transparent. So, it is best to leave each layer of paint to dry before you add the next layer. If you add a layer before the last one has dried, the layers may have moisture trapped between them and produce a cloudy effect.

TAKING IT FURTHER

1 *To create a flatter piece of texture, water the paint down to the consistency of single cream. To stop the paint from running everywhere, outline a shape, in this case a shield, on the glass. Brush the thinned paint into the outline, making sure the it goes right up to the edges. Add a couple more layers of coloured or clear paint.*

2 *When it is dry, just peel the paint away from the glass.*

You can make a number of pieces in the same shape, but with different textures and colours. These look great grouped together on a window.

Coloured thread spirals

There are many types of threads available that can be incorporated into your glass painting. They can be used to add colour and texture to a painted piece of glass, or just to decorate a plain piece.

MATERIALS
Small pot
Water-based glass paints
Water
Paintbrush
Coloured thread
Pen

1 In a small pot, water down some clear paint to the consistency of single cream. Use a brush to push a length of coloured thread right into the thinned paint.

2 Once the thread is coated in paint, place the pot on a sheet of release paper. Lift the end of the thread out of the paint and lay it flat on the paper. Press a flat-ended pen onto the end of the thread and rotate the pen slowly, turning the thread around to start a spiral.

3 Keep spiralling the thread, using the pen to guide the spiral. When it is finished, leave it to dry on the release paper.

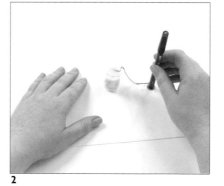

1

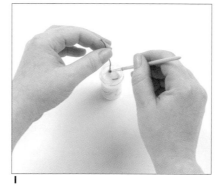

2

3

TAKING IT FURTHER

A length of braid can be formed into a double spiral by twisting each end in turn.

This piece of braid was spiralled around a small square of painted glass.

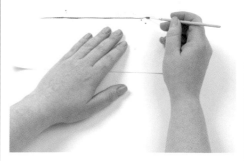

To make a custom- or multi-coloured spiral, lay a length of white thread on release paper and brush it with coloured paints. Spiral it as before.

Wrapping coloured yarn

Thicker yarns and embroidery threads can be applied straight onto a glass item and held in place with clear, or coloured, glass paints. This technique offers a quick and colourful way of adding decoration to a jar or vase, and it is ideal for using up oddments of yarns or cottons left over from other craft projects.

MATERIALS
Glass
Clear water-based glass
  paint
Paintbrush
Coloured yarns
Silicone glue
Cotton spirals

1 Using a thick brush, apply clear paint to the top of the glass, squeezing the paint directly out of the bottle.

2 Paint one section at a time and wrap the yarn over it. The paint will grip the yarn and hold it in place. Build up as many layers of yarn as you wish.

3 When the paint is dry and the yarn is stuck to the glass, apply a coat of clear paint to seal it. Either use a thick brush or fingerpaint it.

4 You can embellish the wrapped glass with cotton spirals (see page 30). Put a blob of silicone glue on the back of each spiral.

5 Stick the spirals to the glass.

1

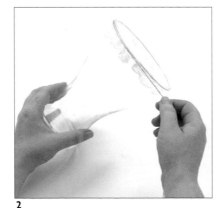

2

3

4

5

Stamping and metal leaf

This technique is so simple, but looks so rich and expensive, and can be incorporated into so many glass painting projects. You will need a sheet of self-adhesive glass painting film for this technique and a pad of archival ink for use on shiny surfaces.

First choose a stamp and lay your film onto a smooth, sturdy, worksurface. Ink up the stamp and stamp cleanly onto the film (see page 12). Use the film economically, getting as many images on it as possible. Let the ink dry; this may take on hour, or you can speed it up with a hairdryer.

MATERIALS
Stamp
Archival ink pad
Self-adhesive glass
   painting film
Scissors
Metal leaf

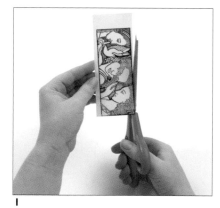

1

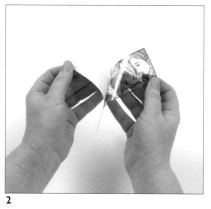

2

1 When the stamp is dry, cut around the design as close to the edge as possible.

2 Peel away the backing sheet, revealing the self-adhesive side, and lay it adhesive-side up on the worksurface.

3 Now lay a sheet of metal carefully over the adhesive side of the film, covering all of the stamped design; if you miss any bits just stick scraps of leaf over them.

4 Press the gold leaf down onto the self-adhesive film, smoothing out any air bubbles.

5 Pull away the excess gold leaf with your fingers, tidying up the edges to produce a clean finish.

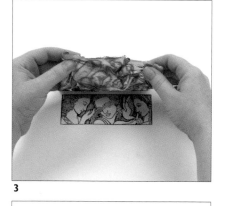

3

4

STICKING THE STAMP
If you wish to stick the gilded stamp to glass, just lightly coat the back with spray glue and stick it straight on to your project. This technique works on painted and unpainted glass, though you cannot wash the glass, just wipe it with a cloth. Save the scraps of leaf produced when tidying up the edges for patching other designs.

5

Sponged and sanded vase

This vase is simple but striking. The contrast between the sponged glass paint and the fine sand gives a bold effect and it is a great example of how two easy techniques can be combined to produce fantastic results.

TECHNIQUES
Masking and sponging, see page 16
Using coloured sand, see page 26

MATERIALS
Tall vase
Royal blue, turquoise, purple, cerise and clear water-based glass paints
Sponge
Sheet of double-sided tape
Scissors
Blue, pink and white sands
Mixing pot
Release paper
Spray varnish

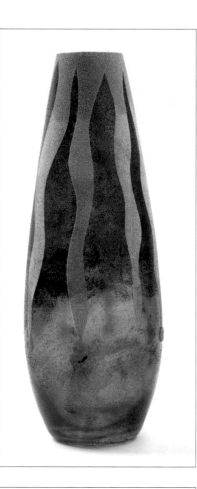

1

2

3

1 Working from the bottom up, sponge royal blue paint one-third of the way up the vase. Sponge turquoise paint above it, blending it into the royal blue.

2 While the paint is still wet, apply the third colour, purple, overlapping and blending it into the turquoise.

3 Finally, sponge on the cerise paint, blending it up to the top of the vase. Place the painted vase to one side to dry, or dry it with a hairdryer.

4 On a sheet of double-sided tape, draw some wavy lines that meet at a point at the bottom, creating wavy triangles approximately three-quarters of the height of the vase. If you top-and-tail them, they will fill the paper with minimum wastage. Cut out the drawn shapes with a pair of scissors.

5 Peel one backing sheet from one shape and, with it just overlapping at the top, stick it to the vase, so that it runs straight down the side. Press it firmly in place.

6 Using a pair of scissors, trim the top of the tape level with the rim of the vase. Peel off the top backing sheet to reveal the other sticky side.

7 Peel one backing sheet off a second shape and stick it next to the first shape, so that they overlap one another a little at the top. Then press it down and remove the other backing sheet. Repeat all the way around the vase. Try not to touch the sticky shapes as your fingers will reduce their stickiness.

8 Cover your worksurface with some paper to catch the sand and help you return it to its container. Starting with the blue sand, sprinkle it around the top of the vase, ensuring that you cover the tops of all the strips of tape.

9 To make the blue sand a lighter colour, mix it with some white sand in a small pot and give it a good shake. Add more white sand if you want a paler colour. Sprinkle the mixed sand over the tape, just below and slightly overlapping the blue.

10 Add some pink sand to the pot of mixed blue and white, give it a good shake and use it to cover the next section of the tape

11 Lastly, cover the lowest part of the tape with plain pink sand. Pat the sand all over with your fingers to help it stick to the tape.

12 Squeeze a blob of clear paint onto a sheet of release paper, then sprinkle blue sand on top. Tip off the excess sand and put to one side to dry, ideally overnight.

13 Put a blob of silicone glue on the back of each blue dot and stick one to the point of each wavy triangle. For added protection, spray the vase lightly with varnish.

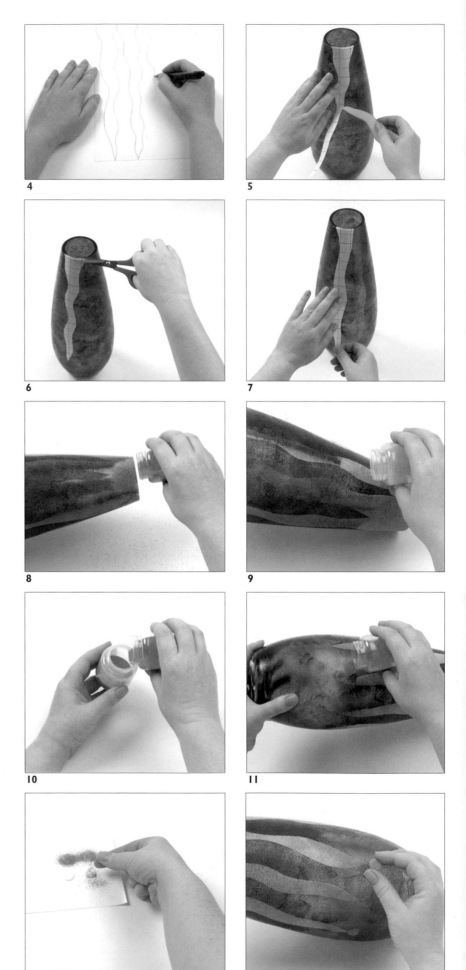

Stencilled egg cupboard

Not only do we use the water-based paint as a glass paint, we use it as a wood stain, too. If you water down the paint a lot – half paint, half water – it gives a nice colourwash effect that tints the surface but doesn't stop the grain of the wood showing through.

1

MATERIALS
Wooden cupboard with
   glass windows
Yellow, light green,
   white, amber and kelly
   green water-based
   glass paints
Mixing pot
Flat paintbrush
Daisy stencil
Low-tack spray glue
Sponges
Hole punch
Paper
Cotton wool bud

TECHNIQUES
Stencilling, see page 20

1 Dilute yellow paint with at least fifty per cent water to make a colourwash that will let the grain of the wood show through.

2 With a wide, flat brush, paint the body of the egg cupboard with yellow and the roof with light green paint.

3 Lightly spray the back of the stencil with low-tack adhesive spray. Position it on the glass and press it down.

4 Stencil the petals of the daisy in white paint with a touch of yellow and the centre with yellow and amber. If a sponge is too big, use a cotton bud to dab the paint on. Repeat the same stencil on the wood of the cupboard.

5 Cut a strip of paper and punch a strip of leaves with a leaf-pattern punch. Space the leaves evenly so that you can stencil the whole strip without having to move it.

6 Spray some low-tack adhesive on the back of the stencil or tape it in place. Sponge the paint onto the leaf stencil, mixing green paints as you go, so you get two-tone leaves.

7 Peel off the stencil. Make a single leaf stencil in the same way and add some random leaves to the roof and sides of the cupboard.

2

3

4

5

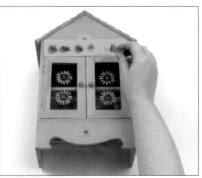

6

7

Rainbow mirror

This is a fun and easy mirror decoration. You start with a basic mirror tile and the bevelled edge is easily done with self-adhesive bevel-effect tape. The fingerpainted film gives the mirror a stained-glass-effect border and we have finished it off with some vinyl designs – butterflies and bugs. Use some double-sided self-adhesive pads to mount the mirror on a wall; make sure you use enough to support the weight of the mirror.

MATERIALS
Mirror tile 30cm (12in)
  square
Self-adhesive bevel-
  effect tape
Metal ruler
Craft knife
Copy glass painting film
Water-based paints in
  your choice of
  colours
Paper trimmer
Rainbow vinyl motifs
Craft knife

TECHNIQUES
Fingerpainting, see page 18
Vinyl outlines, see page 10

Before you start, fingerpaint some copy film in a selection of colours and leave it to dry.

1 Clean the mirror thoroughly. Cut lengths of self-adhesive bevel-effect tape to fit along each side of the mirror. Peel away the backing sheet and stick one length to the mirror. Try to keep your fingers away from the sticky side – you don't want finger prints showing through the tape.

2 Place a metal ruler corner-to-corner across the mirror and cut the tape at an angle with a sharp craft knife.

3 Using a craft knife, remove the excess flap of bevel tape. Repeat the process all the way around until all the sides of mirror are taped.

4 It is important that the strips of fingerpainted film making up the border are all exactly the same width, so use a paper trimmer with a measuring grid to cut them.

5 Cut the strips into various lengths. Peel the backing sheet off the strips one at a time and stick them down, butting them up to the bevel effect tape. Try to alter the lengths to give a patchwork effect.

6 Add a second band of strips of film. Use a craft knife to trim the ends to fit exactly. Add a third band of film in the same way.

7 Stick rainbow vinyl motifs to the mirror, overlapping some of them onto the film border.

1

2

3

4

5

6

7

Star-burst candle lantern

This project is easy to make and stunning to look at. The most time-consuming part is cutting out all the paper masks, but get the children to help and once this is done, the lantern is quick to make.

TECHNIQUES
Masking and sponging, see page 16
Attaching glass decorations,
  see page 25

MATERIALS

Glass candle lantern
Plain paper
Scissors
Spray glue
Turquoise, royal blue,
  purple, gold and
  clear water-based
  glass paints
Paper plate
Sponges

Craft knife
Glass stars
Silicone glue

1 Photocopy a design as many times as you need and cut out the paper masks. Use spray glue to stick the paper to the glass.

2 Sponge on your first colour. Start with the lightest colours first, in this case, turquoise. Do not sponge right up to the rim of the lantern. Work quickly so that the paint doesn't dry before you add the next colour, or the colours won't blend well and you will get hard lines.

3 Sponge royal blue paint around the base of the lantern. This will blend with the turquoise paint to give a graduated colour effect.

4 Using a clean piece of sponge, apply purple paint to the rim of the lantern, overlapping the turquoise paint a little.

5 Using another clean sponge, apply a little gold paint around each of the paper masks, and around the base and rim of the lantern.

6 Use the tip of a craft knife and then your fingers to peel off the paper masks.

7 Finally, using a clean sponge, sponge some clear paint over the clear designs. This will make them look less stark and give a twinkle to the glass when the candlelight shines through them.

8 As a finishing touch, use silicone glue to stick a glass star to the centre of each design.

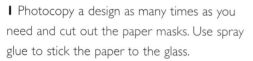
1

2

3

4

5

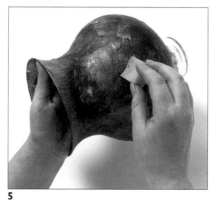
6

7

8

Golden vase

The iridescent gold of the textured

paint and the gilded, stamped

rectangles make this plain glass vase

into a sophisticated centrepiece to

suit the most modern of interiors.

MATERIALS

Sheet of glass or plastic with a textured pattern on it	Ruler
	Craft knife
	Spray glue
Clear and amber water-based glass paints	Feather stamp
	Archival ink pad for stamping onto shiny surfaces
Gold outliner	
Square-sided vase	Self-adhesive glass painting film
Sheet of paper	
Paper trimmer	Gold leaf

1 Fingerpaint the textured glass or plastic with gold outliner and amber paint. When this is dry, fingerpaint a layer of clear paint over the top. Leave to dry and then peel the paint off the surface.

2 Lay the vase on a sheet of paper and draw around it. Cut the shape out.

3 Decide how deep you want the borders around the top and bottom of the vase to be, and then cut the relevant sections off the paper shape to make templates. Use a paper trimmer if you have one or a ruler and a craft knife.

4 Place a template onto the sheet of paint and cut around it with a ruler and craft knife. Make sure when you place the templates on the sheet that the texture is all running the same way. Cut a piece for the top and bottom border on each side of the vase.

5 Coat the backs of all the borders with clear spray glue and stick them to the glass, first do the bottom then the top. If the corners do not stick down neatly, squeeze a little silicone glue in and then press the corners together. Use a strip of masking tape to hold them in place while the glue is drying.

1

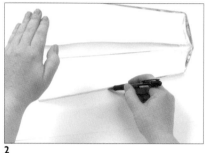

2

4

6

8

TECHNIQUES
Texture from patterned surfaces, see page 28
Stamping and metal leaf, see page 32

3

5

7

9

6 Stamp a feather onto four identically sized pieces of self-adhesive film. Leave to dry.

7 Peel the backing off each stamped piece of film and lay them flat, sticky-side up. Lay a piece of gold leaf over the back of each piece, smooth it down and tidy the edges.

8 Stamp the same feather design

onto the gold leaf, making sure that it is the same way up as the feather on the other side.

9 Coat the gold-leaf side of each stamped piece with spray glue. Position one on each side of the glass vase and pat them down. Make sure that they are in the same position on each side of the vase.

In this chapter of the book you will find techniques and projects that should take an hour or so to complete, depending on how quickly you work, of course. Some projects have longer preparation time, but the actual techniques used are quick to do and all the projects are easy to assemble.

in an hour

outlining

Traditional outlining

The outline is the skeleton of your work. It forms the pattern and prevents the paints from running into each other. If you want to be good at outlining you must put in a little practice. It is well worth it to make your projects look good.

MATERIALS
Outliner
Glass

1

2

3

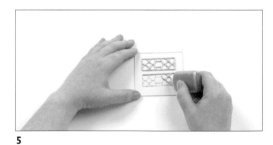

4

5

1 Just touch the glass with the tip of the bottle and gently squeeze, then lift the outliner up as it comes out.
2 Keeping the outliner just off the glass, move the bottle, and the outliner, to draw a line.
3 Your accuracy and control is much greater if you keep the bottle's nozzle lifted off the glass.
4 To finish the line, stop squeezing, lay the outliner on the glass, touch the glass gently and take the nozzle away.
5 To outline a specific design, lay a paper template under the glass and outline over the top. It is helpful if the template is a different colour to the outliner, as it makes it easy to see where you are in the design.

SUCCESSFUL OUTLINING

Keep the bottles of outliner upside down in a cup, then the nozzle will stay moist and not dry up. Also, the outliner will always be ready to use, with no air bubbles which could splatter all over your project.

While you are working, keep a folded piece of kitchen towel by your side and wipe any blobs of outliner off the tip of the bottle as, when and if they occur.

Outliner lines on release paper

If your outlining has got to the stage where you are confident with a straight line, but find curves and detail a problem, this could be the technique for you. You simply need to produce a reasonably straight line onto a piece of release paper, the shaping is done once the outliner is dry.

MATERIALS
Outliner
Release paper
Glass

1 Outline some lines onto a sheet of release paper. Leave them to dry.
2 When they are dry you can peel the lines off.
3 The lines are very malleable and can be bent into any shape you want. Pat them down onto the glass and they will cling there, Use scissors to cut the lines to length and paint the designs in the usual way.

TAKING IT FURTHER
You can make instant coloured designs by laying outliner on to coloured or painted glass.

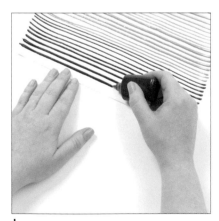

1

2

3

Colour with outliner

This is the simplest way to create an instant, coloured design: coloured outliner on coloured glass, no painting needed. Outline the design onto release paper and then, when it is dry, peel it off and stick it onto the glass. We have used gold outliner, but some water-based paints can be turned into outliner by adding a thickening agent to them. This gives you a great range of coloured outliners to choose from.

Small designs are easy to peel and stick, but the bigger the design, the greater the risk of it tangling up as you peel it off the release paper.

MATERIALS

Release paper
Gold outliner
Craft knife
Coloured glass

1

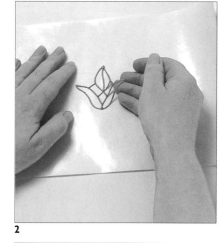

2

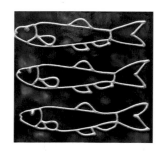

3

1 Place a design under a piece of release paper and outline over the lines. Leave the outliner to dry.
2 Carefully peel the design off the release paper. Use a craft knife to lift one corner of the outliner and then peel it off with your fingers.
3 Lay the design in position on the coloured glass and gently pat it down.

PEELING OFF THE DESIGN

Turn the release paper over and peel the design off upside down, letting it fall onto a piece of kitchen towel. This helps to prevent larger designs from tangling and allows the design to spring back into shape if it has stretched slightly when being peeled off.

TAKING IT FURTHER

Choose an coloured outliner to suit the design: these silver fish on deep-blue glass look suitably maritime.

Rather than buying coloured glass, you can paint a piece of clear glass with glass paints, and when it is dry, apply the outlined design.

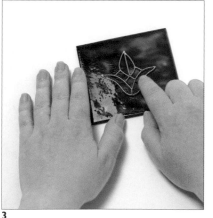

Dripping

Water-based glass paint can be thinned to make it drip easily and allow you to achieve various effects. You can dribble it in thin streams to give a ribbed effect. You can splodge it onto glass to create a wide ribbon. You can drip one layer of paint, let it dry and then drip the next layer over the top

MATERIALS
Water-based glass paints
Paintbrush
Glass

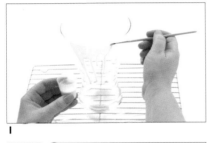

1

2

3

1 When you have watered down the paints to the consistency you want to work with, (the thickness of single cream will allow it to flow easily) hold your paint pot up to the glass and with a brush, drip clear paint down the glass. This will add texture and help the colours to flow.

2 While the clear paint is still wet, dribble coloured paint over the glass. Leave this layer to dry to dry.

3 Build up layers of colours, ensuring that you cover the glass evenly. Leave each layer to dry before adding the next one.

SUCCESSFUL DRIPPING

Stand the glass on a wire baking tray over a plate so that as the drips run down they do not pool around the base of the glass. If, once it has dried, the paint has stuck the glass to the wire tray, just cut it away with a craft knife.

You can use a hairdryer to dry the paint between layers. Be careful not to blow your dribbles to one side and if you blow dry from the bottom, always keep the hairdryer at arms length away from the drips. We tend to start with paler colours and drip darker colours over them, but this depends on the project. You can drip a few colours at once so that the paints mix and make their own colours: if you add clear paint it will make colours paler.

Scraffito

This is an ancient ceramic technique that can be applied to glass painting. It works best if you paint a light colour first and a darker colour on top, so that when you scrape away the dark colour the light one shows through. But it does work the other way around if you know how to mix colours. If you paint a blue layer first, then apply a yellow layer, you will be left with yellow and green lines when you scrape through; the yellow on the blue will make green. Try yellow on red to make orange, or red on blue to make purple.

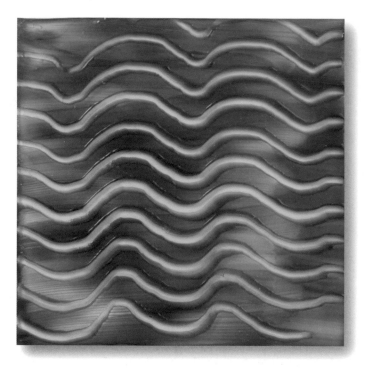

MATERIALS
Card
Decorative-edge
  scissors
Painted glass
Water-based glass
  paints in two colours

TAKING IT FURTHER
Different combs used with different motions will produce very distinctive patterns on the glass. Experiment with items such as hair combs and forks to see what you can achieve.

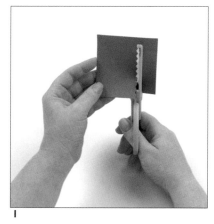

1

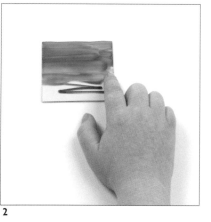

2

3

1 Using decorative-edge scissors, cut across a piece of thin card to make a comb.

2 With your finger or a brush apply a second colour to a dry, painted piece of glass.

3 Applying light pressure, drag the card comb across the glass, exposing the colour underneath.

Metallic paints

Metallic paints can give some interesting effects, so try to incorporate them into some of your glass painting projects. They look great when painted over glass paint, or when used just to add a highlight or two to a project painted in plain colours. When the metallics catch the light they really make the details sing out. Glass paints are also available in pearl and lustre finishes, both of which can be used in the same way.

MATERIALS
Glass
Metallic outliner
Metallic paints
Paintbrush

1 A design can be outlined in gold or silver and then painted with metallic paints. Apply the paints in the same way as conventional glass paints, painting one section at a time and brushing the paint right up to the edges of the outline. Try blending different colours to create some stunning effects.

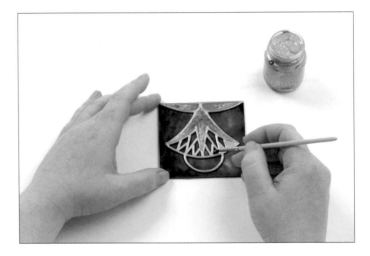

TAKING IT FURTHER

This silver moon and stars were outlined in silver and then the back of the glass was sprayed with a chrome paint.

Here the same silver moon, but without stars, was outlined onto a background painted with blue metallic paints.

This leaf was made by outlining a leaf shape in gold onto self-adhesive film. When dry the leaf was cut out, the backing peeled off and gold leaf stuck to the sticky back.

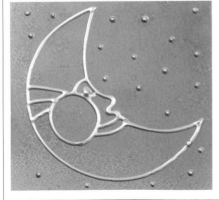

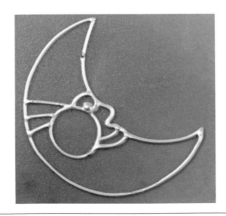

Oriental lacquer effect

The images will stand out very boldly using this technique. What works really well is to paint a bold design on the outside of a glass vase, then spray the inside of the vase in a contrasting colour. The traditional colours are red, black and gold, but there is no reason why you shouldn't experiment with other colours. Car spray paints work well and they are available in an enormous range of colours.

MATERIALS
Gold outliner
Gold water-based glass
    paint
Glass
Red spray paint

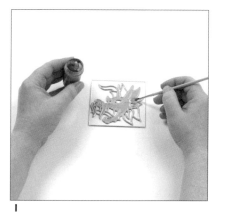

1

2

1 Outline the design in gold and leave it to dry. Water down some gold glass paint or use a metallic paint and paint the design.
2 When the design is dry, turn the glass over and spray the back with red paint.

TAKING IT FURTHER

Red outliner with a black background gives a sophisticated effect.

A black outlined flower is very graphic against a plain gold background.

52

Spraying layers

You can spray water-based paint by thinning it and pouring it into a plastic spray bottle, which are available in craft stores. You need to water down the paint enough so that it sprays easily through the nozzle of the bottle. Choose a bottle with a cap to prevent the nozzle from drying out and getting blocked.

MATERIALS
Spray bottle
Water-based glass paint
Water
Glass
Sheet of paper

1 Squeeze some of the water-based paint into a spray bottle.

2 Add some water to the paint to achieve a consistency that will allow you to spray the paint easily through the nozzle. If it is too thick, just add a bit more water.

3 Replace the cap and the lid and give the bottle a good shake to mix the water and paint together. This will also create some air bubbles, so let the paint rest for a few minutes to allow the bubbles to disperse.

4 Put some paper over the worksurface to protect it. Lay the glass on the worksurface and then lay the sheet of paper on top of the glass. Hold your spray bottle about 30cm (12in) or so away from the glass and spray lightly.

5 To keep the colours more defined, it's best to dry the first paint layer with a hairdryer before you go on to spray the next layer.

6 Reposition the paper and spray the second colour, then move the paper again and spray a third colour.

7 Remove the paper completely and spray a final layer of colour.

1

2

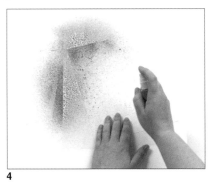
3

4

5

6

7

CLEANING THE SPRAY

To clean your spray bottles empty out any excess paint and wash the bottle with water. Then fill it with water and spray through the nozzle until the water sprays clean. If you don't do this the nozzle will become blocked and the spray useless.

Masking and spraying

There are many different spray paints offering various paint effects. Spray glass paints in various colours, stone effect paints, metal, cracked, frosted and pearl spray paints are all available. Most of the sprays can be sprayed directly onto glass, though some may advise a primer first, check the details on the can. You need good ventilation when spraying, read the instructions on each type of can and always follow the safety directives.

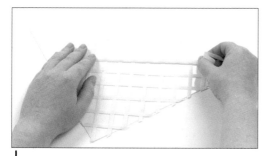

1

MATERIALS
Glass
Masking tape
Spray paint

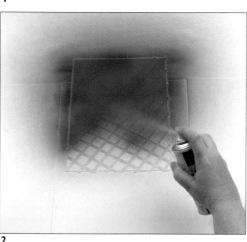

2

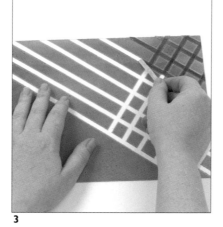

3

TAKING IT FURTHER

You can also cut out masks from wide masking tape or paper with a low-tack spray glue on the back. Stick the design to the glass, then spray and peel off the mask. This flower design was made with a paper mask stuck to a piece of blue glass that was sprayed silver.

1 You can buy masking tape in a variety of different widths; choose a low-tack tape that will peel off easily. Mask off your glass or film with tape. You can place a design under the glass and follow that if you wish. Make sure that the tape is pressed down firmly so that the paint does not run under it.

2 Following the instructions on the can, hold it at the right distance from the glass and lightly spray the paint.

3 When the paint is dry, peel off the tape.

SUCCESSFUL SPRAYING

Peel tape back on itself at a tight angle so that it cuts through the paint. This gives a sharp edge to the paint. If you just lift the tape up it may lift the paint and give it a rough edge.

You can use a big cardboard box on its side to act as a spray cabinet and help to stop the spray going everywhere. Just place your project in the box and spray.

Stained glass mosaic

This is an easy technique that gives fantastic results. Cut out the squares carefully so that they are all the same size; you can photocopy a grid onto the back of self-adhesive copy film then when it is fingerpainted and dry, you just cut up the grid.

MATERIALS
Sheets of self-adhesive
   copy film fingerpainted
   in various colours
Scissors
Glass

1

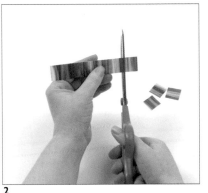

2

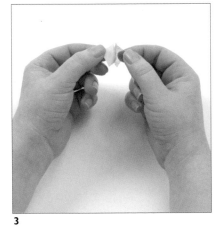

3

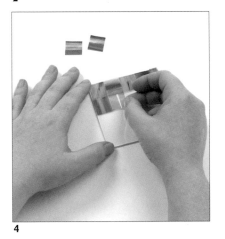

4

1 Cut fingerpainted film into strips.
2 Then cut the strips into squares.
3 Peel the backing sheet off each square as you need it.
4 Stick the film onto the glass randomly or into a pattern. If you alter the direction of the grain of the paint as you stick the squares down you will get a checkerboard effect.

TAKING IT FURTHER

Cut strips of the painted film and stick them in a grid pattern over the joins between the squares for a contemporary finish.

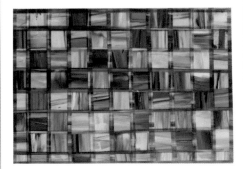

For a more traditional look, use self-adhesive lead to delineate the squares in the mosaic (see page 82)

Embedding beads

Beads come in all shapes, sizes and colours and will add a fantastic jewel-like quality to your designs. The pieces shown here are made with loose beads, but you can also incorporate beads on a string or beaded fringing into glass painting projects.

MATERIALS
Self-adhesive glass
   painting film
Outliner
Clear water-based glass
   paint
Paintbrush
Beads of various colours
   and sizes
Scissors

1 Outline your chosen design onto self-adhesive film and leave it to dry. Using gold or silver outliner will add to the final effect.

2 Squeeze a drop of clear water-based glass paint into each section of the outlined design.

3 With a small paintbrush, spread the paint right up to the outliner.

4 Two large clear beads make the eyes for this dragonfly. Just place them into the paint in the right position.

5 For the dragonfly's body use iridescent blue/green beads. Sprinkle them over the whole body. Work quickly so that the beads embed into the paint before it dries. Any stray beads can be picked up on the tip of the paintbrush and carefully moved into the body sections of the dragonfly.

6 Water down some clear paint to the consistency of single cream and gently brush it over the beads to help hold them in position.

7 When the body is dry, repeat the process with the wings, using translucent pearl beads. Let the whole dragonfly dry.

8 Carefully cut out the design with sharp scissors or place it on a cutting mat and cut it out with a craft knife.

9 Peel the backing paper off the dragonfly and stick it onto the glass.

MATCHING COLOURS
If you want to bead an area of a project and would like the colour to match another painted area, simply embed clear beads into the appropriate coloured paint.

1

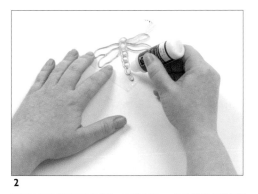

2

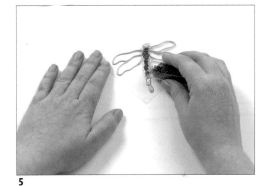

3

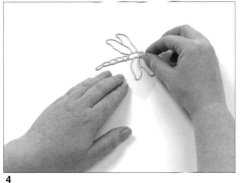

4

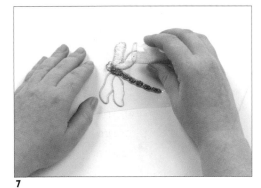

5

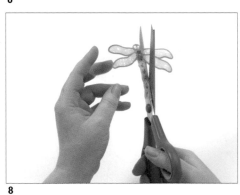

6

7

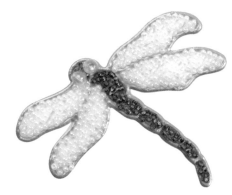

8

9

TAKING IT FURTHER

Your can make beaded designs as elaborate as painted ones, but the separate areas of the design must be large enough to hold a reasonable quantity of beads.

Designs don't have to be pictorial, geometric ones work just as well.

Embedding sequins

You can get some quick decorative effects just by embedding materials into your paint. Sequins are ideal as they are available in many different colours and designs. However, you do need to use a water-based paint with sequins, as solvent-based paints bleed the colour out of them.

Materials
Clear water-based glass
  paint
Sequins
Glass

1

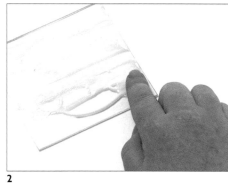

2

1 Doodle some paint onto the glass.

2 Use your finger or a paintbrush to spread the paint in a thin, even layer across the glass.

3 While the paint is still wet, drop your sequins into it. If one falls in the wrong place, you can move it with the tip of a cocktail stick. Leave the paint to dry.

4 Doodle more paint over the top of the sequins and spread it out in a thin layer, as before.

3

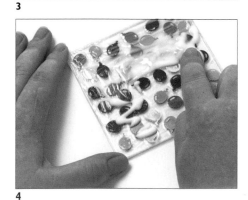

4

TAKING IT FURTHER
You can use any shaped sequins in this way, and if you embed them onto thick film, you can use them as inserts in greetings cards.

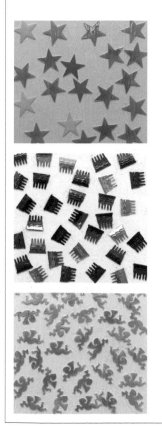

Spun glass

This is such a simple technique, but it looks wonderfully effective. It works best on round glass objects, and if you choose the colours well the end result can look just like an expensive, designer-made piece.

Materials
Water-based glass paints
   in your chosen colours
Release paper
Glass

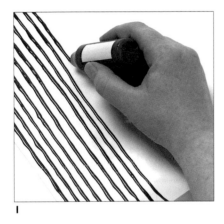

1

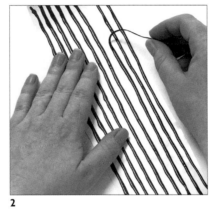

2

3

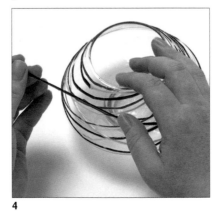

4

1 Use the paint straight from the bottle and streak lines onto a piece of release paper. Don't make the lines too thin or they will break when you peel them off. Leave them to dry.
2 One by one, peel the lines of paint off the paper.
3 If a line of paint has a thick blob on one end, pull it off.
Press the end of a line onto the glass, it will stick by itself.
4 Hold the line of paint taut in your left hand and wind it around the glass, pressing it down with your right hand. Stretching the line gently as you press it down will ensure that it sticks firmly and evenly.

TAKING IT FURTHER

You can also sprinkle various materials into the paint while it is still wet. Try fine sand, which you can buy in various colours, or glitter, or even a very fine glass granules, as shown here, which look like sugar.

Embedding fabric

Fabrics are a wonderful way of very quickly adding decoration to plain glass. For a wedding use offcuts of the bride's lace or the bridesmaid's dresses to decorate placements and invitations and to make table decorations. For thin, fine fabrics use the paint straight from the bottle – this will stop the fabric bubbling. For thicker fabrics, water down the water-based paint with one part water to one part paint. Thicker fabrics do not tend to bubble and the thinner paint will soak into them more easily.

MATERIALS
Clear water-based glass
  paint
Flat paintbrush
Self-adhesive film
Fabric
Rubber stamp
Archival ink pad
Sharp scissors
Glass

1 Using a flat paintbrush, brush some clear paint (in this case straight from the bottle as we are using a fine fabric) onto self-adhesive film.

2 Cut a piece of fabric slightly larger than the sheet of film and lay it down over the wet paint. Gently pull the edges to smooth out creases.

3 Squeeze a little more paint into the centre of the fabric and brush it out across the whole sheet, working from the centre out. Brush out any air bubbles as you go. Leave the paint to dry overnight.

4 The paint will be absorbed into the fibres of the fabric and when it is dry the fabric will be completely stuck to the film. If you have used film with a paper backing, you can draw a design onto the backing, cut it out and then peel the backing off and stick the film to glass, paper, ceramic or any other smooth surface.

5 To rubber stamp onto the fabric, just ink up your stamp and press down. Lift up the stamp cleanly and leave the ink to dry.

6 Cut out the stamped design with sharp scissors, cutting as close as possible to the edges.

7 Peel the backing off the film, exposing the sticky side.

8 Stick the stamped fabric onto your chosen surface.

1

2

3

4

5

6

7

8

SUCCESSFUL EMBEDDING

Most fabrics can be used with this technique, but watch out for any which have been treated; for example, those impregnated with oil for a wipe-down tablecloth will not work.

The different films available for glass painting work well with the fabric technique. Use self-adhesive films, either a plain film or a copy film, if you want to cut out a particular design to embellish a piece of glass. Thick film will make wonderful fabric cards or mobiles and extra-thick film can be used to make items such as clocks.

Colouring fabric

This is a variation on the technique of embedding

fabric and allows you to colour a plain white or cream

fabric to match or tone with other sections of a

painted glass project.

MATERIALS
Water-based glass paints
Flat paintbrush
Self-adhesive film
Fabric
Motif
Sharp scissors
Glass

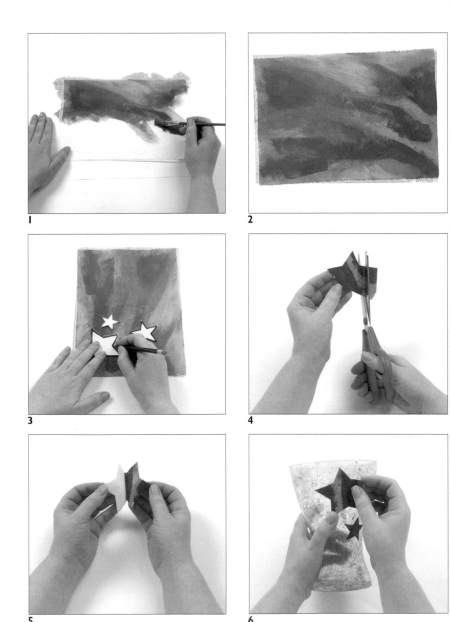

I Fix plain white fabric to film with a thin layer of clear water-based paint, as described in Embedding Fabric (see page 60). Then, paint over the fabric with water-based paints in the colours of your choice. Either paint the whole sheet with one colour or blend different colours together as you paint them on.

2 Leave the finished piece of painted fabric to dry.

3 To make fabric motifs, you can embed the fabric onto copy film and draw the designs on the back. However, if you want to use a specific piece of the painted fabric, make a paper template, lay it in position on the surface of the fabric and draw around it with a pencil.

4 Cut out the motifs with scissors.

5 Peel off the backing sheet to expose the self-adhesive side of the film.

6 Stick the motifs onto glass, or any other smooth surface. Here the motifs have been stuck to a toning sponged vase.

Layering paper

There are some fantastic papers on the market now, many of which can be incorporated into your glass painting projects to give some interesting finishes and textures. If you are using coloured and patterned papers, use clear glass paint. With the white and cream colours, you can use any combination of coloured paints.

MATERIALS
Water-based glass paints
Flat paintbrush
Glass
Paper

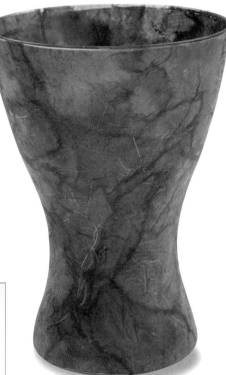

1

2

3

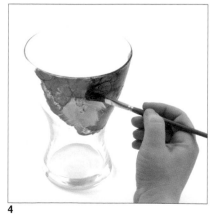
4

5

1 Water down water-based glass paint to the consistency of single cream and paint some onto a small area of the glass.

2 Rip up the paper into random-sized pieces. We have used a thin, hand-made paper. Keep the pieces with the original straight edges in a separate pile; these are placed around the edges of the glass to give a neat finish.

Lay a piece of paper over the wet paint on the glass and pat it down with a paintbrush. The paint will soak into the paper and stick to the glass.

3 Paint over the paper with more watered-down paint.

4 Paint more sections and add more pieces of paper, blending paint colours together as you work. If you are working on a vase, as shown here, work from the top downwards, using some straight-edged pieces of paper for the rim and saving the rest for the base.

5 If you find a gap then just lay another piece of paper over it and paint it down as before.

Polymer clay decorations

You can use either air-drying or oven-bake clays to make these decorations; we have even used salt-dough to make embellishments for glass projects. You can either make motifs, like those shown here, or use thin strips of clay to make patterns on the glass.

MATERIALS
Polymer clay
Cookie cutter
Egg box
Water-based glass paints
  or metallic paints
Paintbrush
Silicone glue
Glass

1 Take a small piece of clay and roll it into a ball. Use the palm of your hand or a rolling pin to flatten it out to a disc of the thickness you require. If the clay is sticky, sprinkle a little talcum powder on the surface.

2 Use a cookie cutter to stamp shapes out of the clay. You can also cut out your own designs with a craft knife, though this can be quite fiddly to do.

3 Gently push the clay shape out of the cookie cutter.

4 You can leave the clay on a piece of paper to dry flat, or you can give it some shape. To do this, leave it to dry on something like an egg box or the inside of a cardboard tube.

5 To add colour to the shapes, just paint them with water-based glass paints or metallic paints.

6 To stick the clay decorations to glass, just put a blob of silicone glue on the back of each one.

7 Stick the shape to the glass and, if necessary, use a strip of masking tape to hold it in place while it dries.

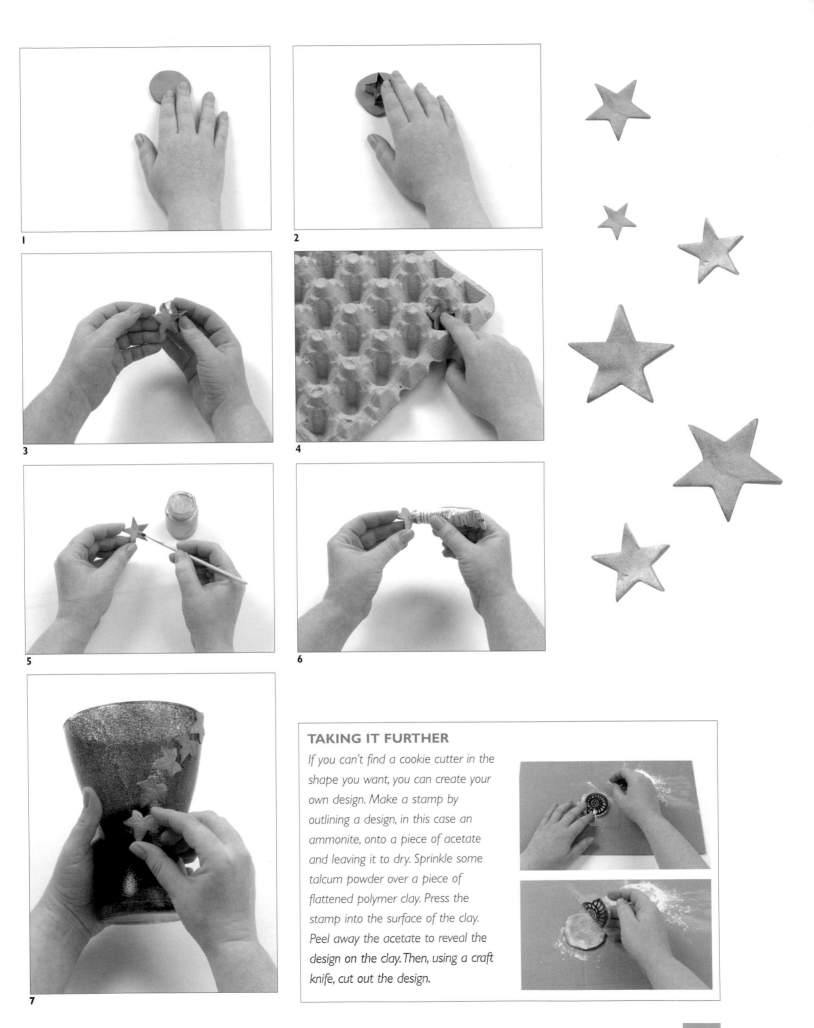

1

2

3

4

5

6

TAKING IT FURTHER

If you can't find a cookie cutter in the shape you want, you can create your own design. Make a stamp by outlining a design, in this case an ammonite, onto a piece of acetate and leaving it to dry. Sprinkle some talcum powder over a piece of flattened polymer clay. Press the stamp into the surface of the clay. Peel away the acetate to reveal the design on the clay. Then, using a craft knife, cut out the design.

7

Spiral lamp

All you need for this project is a good eye when sticking the masking tape spiral to the glass. We have used yellow and orange spray paints, but, of course, you can use any colour scheme you want. A turntable is useful, but you can stand the lamp on a small table and walk around it instead.

MATERIALS
Cylinder lamp
Plastic bag
Masking tape
Sheet of paper
Spray glass paints in
 orange and yellow

TECHNIQUES
Masking and spraying, see page 54

I To protect the flex and plug from the spray paint, put them into a plastic bag and tape it up tightly. Tape over the remaining flex where it meets the lamp.

2 Starting at the top of the lamp, stick down the masking tape so that it goes over the rim. Start sticking the tape around the lamp – you have to do this by eye. You want an even spiral: if it looks uneven, unwrap the tape and re-align it.

3 To stop the paint getting into the inside of the lamp, take a big sheet of paper and roll it up. Place it in the top of the lamp and let it unfurl so that it fits snugly inside the rim.

4 Protect the worksurface. Always read the instructions on the can before you start and work in a well-ventilated area, preferably outdoors. Spray the lamp with orange paint, using smooth, sweeping strokes to cover random sections of the glass. Spray yellow paint in the areas left plain. Allow the colours to overlap a little so that they blend smoothly.

5 Starting at the top of the lamp, peel off the masking tape. Peel the tape back on itself so that it cuts through the paint, giving a clean, sharp edge to the lines.

Oriental candle sconce

This striking dragon design would really set the scene in an oriental-style room. The back is lightly sprayed with gold glitter paint, not solid gold, so that when the candle is lit the gold flecks twinkle in the light. This design would also look good on the back of a glass plate.

MATERIALS
Glass candle sconce
Black outliner
Red solvent-based glass
  paint
Paintbrush
Gold speckled spray
  paint

TECHNIQUES
Traditional outlining, see page 46
Masking and spraying, see page 54

1

2

3

4

1 Place the design under the glass and outline it with black outliner. Start at the centre of the design and work your way out to the edges of the glass. You could use gold or silver outliner if you prefer.

2 When the outliner is dry, you can paint the dragon. Choose a strong colour – this dragon is red – and a solvent-based paint for the maximum amount of translucency.

3 Leave the dragon to dry overnight.

4 When the paint is dry, turn the glass over and spray the back with a gold glitter spray paint. Remember to read the instructions on the can, spray in a well-ventilated area and to protect your worksurface.

Textured mosaic panel

This panel is a kind of sampler of many of the different fast glass painting techniques explained in this book. Here the panel is mounted in a frame and hung on the wall like a picture, but it would also look fantastic in a window with the light shining through it. Look at cross-stitch designs for inspiration for your own panels; they are already made up from small squares so a lot of the work has been done for you.

TECHNIQUES
Crackle effect, see page 23
Using coloured sand, see page 26
Metallic paints, see page 51
Embedding sequins, see page 58
Stained glass mosaic, see page 55
Outlining with self-adhesive lead,
  see page 82

MATERIALS

Various painted and textured sheets of self-adhesive film	Scissors
	Sticky tape
Glass or extra thick film the size of the finished panel	3mm (⅛in) and 6mm (¼in) brass-coloured self-adhesive lead
2 sheets of squared or graph paper	

1 Work out your design on a sheet of squared paper the same size as your piece of glass. Choose squared paper with squares about 1cm (½in) in size. If they are smaller than this, the film becomes very fiddly to work with. To make an abstract panel, cut shapes out of another sheet of squared paper and lay them onto the main sheet. When you are happy with the design, tape them in place.

2 Lay the sheet of glass or extra-thick film over the design.

3 Cut the sheets of film into squares the same size as those on the squared paper. If you are making a big panel it is well worth cutting up all the sheets before you start and putting each one into a separate small plastic bag. This way you have a supply of all the colours and textures you want: put a good film on the television and sit and snip.

4 Peel the backing paper off the squares one at a time.

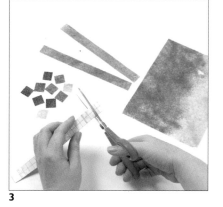

1

3

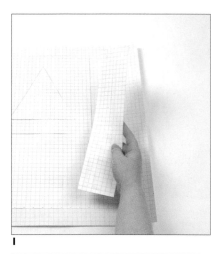

4

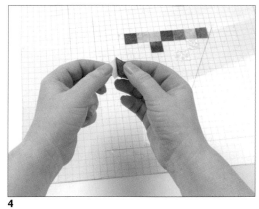

5

5 Choose which part of the design you want to work on first. Then choose the colours and textures you want to use and start sticking down the squares, following the design under the glass. Stick the squares on carefully for a neat mosaic.

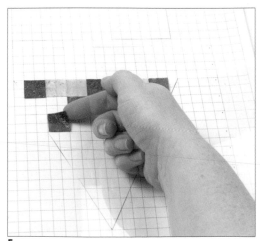

5

PAINTED AND TEXTURED FILM

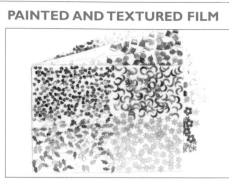

Various glitter flakes and sequins embedded onto sheets of self-adhesive film.

Sheets of self-adhesive film covered with coloured sands and fine granules.

Sheets of self-adhesive film sprayed with flecked and crackle finishes.

Sheets of self adhesive film sprayed with metallic finishes

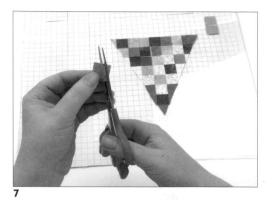

6

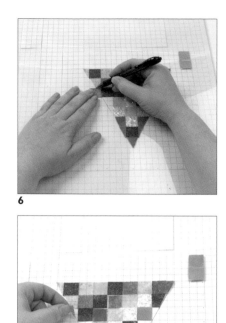

7

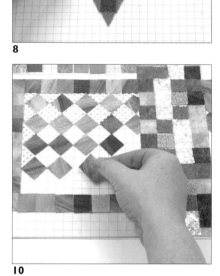

8

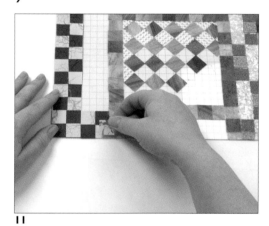

9

10

11

12

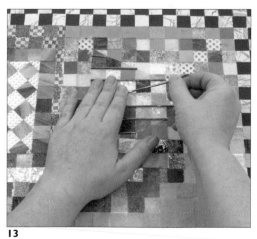

13

6 If you are working on shapes that are not square, in this case a triangle, you will have to cut the painted squares to fit. To do this lay the square down where you want the final piece to be, without removing the backing paper. Make a tiny pen mark on either side of the square where the outside edge of the triangle bisects it.

7 Cut from mark to mark with scissors, producing a piece of painted film the size you need.

8 Stick the shape down in the right place.

9 Build up the design section by section, completing each element of the design before moving on to the next one.

10 You can add an extra dimension to your mosaic by turning some squares onto their corners to make diamonds and filling in an element of the design with them.

11 A border is a good compositional element in any design, though you can allow some of the internal elements to break through it for a dynamic effect.

12 Stick down squares until you have covered the whole design.

13 In this panel all the squares are outlined with 3mm (⅛in) lead and the separate elements of the design are outlined with 6mm (¼in) lead.

Working in one segment at a time and starting with the 3mm (⅛in) lead, stick it down over the longest straight lines first, running one length of lead across as many squares as possible. When you have leaded all the necessary lines running in one direction, lead all the perpendicular lines.

14 Work methodically, leading all the elements and doing the background last.

15 The 6mm (¼in) lead is used to define the main elements within the panel and to frame the border.

Once you have stuck all the lead in place, rub it down with the end of a plastic pen.

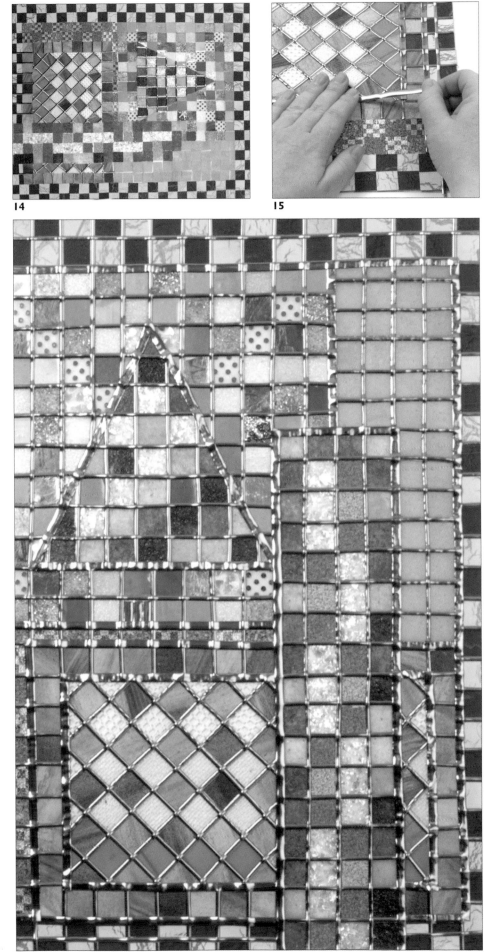

14

15

13

Fossil bowl

This project involves a number of different techniques, all combined to make this Jurassic bowl. Once each element has been made up, combining them is a quick and easy task. If you prefer, you can speed the process up by leaving out one of the techniques.

MATERIALS

Ammonite rubber
  stamp
Archival ink pad
White hand-made
  thin paper
Glass bowl
Water-based metallic
  paints in green,
  amber, gold, bronze,
  purple, turquoise.
Flat paintbrush
Air-drying polymer clay
Talcum powder
Black outliner
Acetate
Sheet of cardboard
Silicone glue
Water-based glass paints
  in clear, light green,
  kelly green, amber,
  aqua and yellow.

TECHNIQUES

Stamping an outline, see page 12
Layering paper, see page 63
Polymer clay decorations, see page 64
Traditional outlining, see page 46
Fingerpainting, see page 18
Dripping, see page 49

1

2

3

4

5

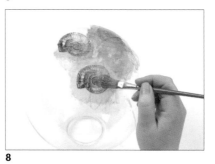

6

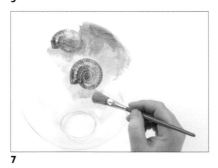

7

8

1 Sprinkle some talcum powder onto a piece of cardboard. Make a small clay disc and press both sides of it into the talc.

2 Make a stamp template by stamping the rubber stamp onto paper. Lay the acetate over it and outline the ammonite design. Leave it it to dry. Press the stamp into the surface of the clay.

3 Peel away the acetate to reveal the design in the clay. Then, using a craft knife, cut out the design.

4 Gently press the clay ammonites onto the bowl you are using and leave them to dry. This way, when you come to stick them onto the bowl, they will have the correct curve and will sit neatly on the glass. The clay will drop off when dry, so

stand bowl on something soft; a towel is ideal.

5 Stamp the hand-made paper with the ammonite rubber stamp using an ink or paint which will not run when wet. Leave it to dry.

6 Tear out the stamped images.

7 Layer stamped images and plain paper onto the glass, using the metallic paints to hold them in place and colour them at the same

time. Turn the bowl upside down and, starting at the base, work down the sides.

8 Blend the different paint colours as you work.

9

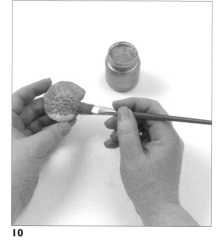

10

11

12

13

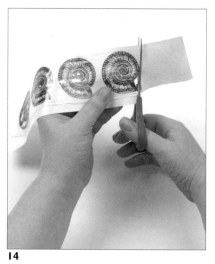

14

9 Continue adding paper until you have covered about half of the bowl. Leave it upside down to dry.

10 When the clay ammonites are dry, paint them with metallic paints.

11 When all the paint is dry, stick the clay ammonites to the papered part of the glass with silicone glue.

12 Layer some more paper over parts of the clay ammonites, so that they look as though they are embedded in the paper.

13 Make a sheet of clear paint film by fingerpainting clear paint onto release paper. Once the paint is dry, stamp it with the ammonite stamp.

14 Cut out the ammonites with scissors, leaving the backing in place.

15 Peel off the backing and lay the paint ammonites on the glass; they will cling there by themselves.

16 Drip clear and then yellow paint down the sides of the bowl. Use

15

16

quite a lot of paint to create strong dripped lines.

17 Allow the yellow to dry and then drip amber paint. Finally, when the amber is dry, drip turquoise paint.

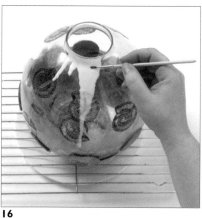

17

Beaded rainbow catcher

Hang this rainbow catcher in a window and when the sun shines through the crystal in the centre, rainbows will appear all over the walls of the room. It is best to make these catchers from rigid, extra thick, plastic film, as glass would be very difficult to cut to shape. Choose translucent and iridescent beads that will catch the sunlight.

TECHNIQUES
Traditional outlining, see page 46
Embedding beads, see page 56

MATERIALS

Sheet of extra thick film	Clear, pale pink, bright pink, gold, purple and blue beads
Gold outliner	
Scissors	
Hot stencil cutter	Silicone glue
Clear water-based glass paint	Round crystal to fit the hole in the design
Fine paintbrush	Nylon thread

I The extra thick film comes with a protective backing sheet. Peel this off at least one hour before you want to outline onto it. If you don't do this, the static electricity caused by taking the backing sheet off will make your outliner jump all over the place.

I

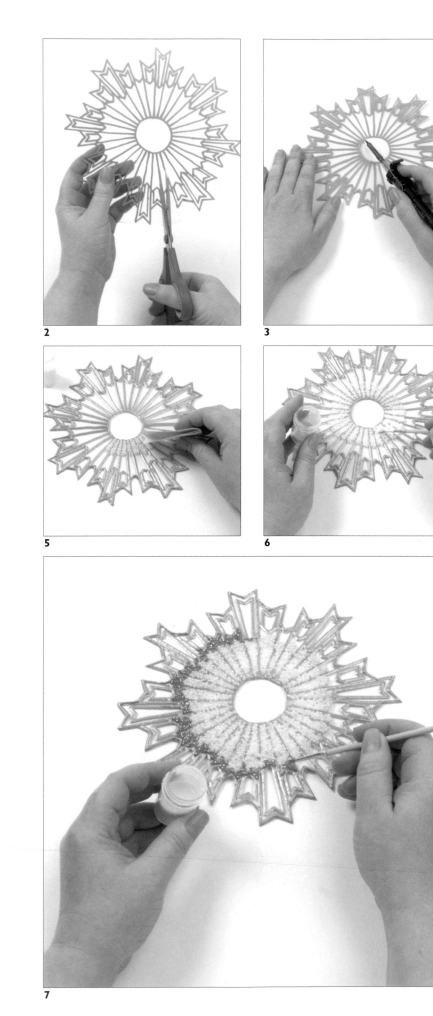

2

3

4

5

6

7

2 Place your design under the film and outline it in gold. Leave it to dry and then cut the shape out with sturdy scissors.

3 Use a hot stencil cutter to cut out the circle in the middle of the design. It is a good idea at this time to check that the crystal fits the hole; it should sit in it without falling right through.

4 Starting in the middle, brush clear paint into a few sections of the design. Try not to get paint on the gold outliner or the beads will stick to it and the gold won't show.

5 Drop clear beads onto the paint. If you fold a strip of paper in half and decant a small amount of beads into this it makes it easier to drop them in the right spot. When you have beaded a few sections, paint a few more and then bead them. Work right around the design in this way.

6 When all beads are in position, drop some clear paint over them to help hold them in place. Leave to dry for a short while.

7 Add the pale pink beads in the same way. Use the tip of you paintbrush to nudge any stray beads into the right place. Next, add the bright pink beads and leave them to dry. A hair dryer can be used to speed up the drying time, but don't hold it too close, as you don't want to blow the beads away.

8 Next add the gold beads, followed by the purple beads. Finally add the blue beads. Leave to dry completely.

9 Place the beaded film over a cup and place the crystal in the hole. Squeeze some silicone glue into an outlining bag and pipe it around the base of the crystal, so that the glue touches the crystal and the film. Leave to dry. When the glue is dry, turn the rainbow catcher over and silicone the back of the crystal in the same way. Leave to dry.

10 Then with a bradawl or hot stencil cutter, make a small hole at the top of the rainbow catcher. Push some nylon thread through the hole to hang the rainbow catcher from.

8

9

10

In this chapter you will find techniques and projects that take more time to complete. However, they are speedy variations of some of the traditional glass painting techniques and can be done in an afternoon. You can simplify some of the projects by using less complex designs.

in an afternoon

outlining

Outlining with self-adhesive lead

Lead can be used in various ways, but this technique offers a way of outlining a design simply and quickly. It is an ideal technique for those who love painting but find outlining more difficult. Use lead of a width that is appropriate to your design.

MATERIALS
Glass
Water-based glass paints
Paintbrush
3mm (⅛in) self-adhesive
  lead
Plastic pen

WORKING WITH LEAD
Lead should be safety-coated so that you do not get any residue on your fingers when you work with it. If you are unsure as to whether the lead you are using is coated, wear gloves when working and wash your hands before touching your face or any food. Keep the glass dry so that the lead sticks to it well.

1 Lay a template under glass and paint in the major elements. As there is no outliner, paint carefully, as close to the edges of the design as possible. Leave the paint to dry.

2 Keeping the template under the glass, start leading the shorter lines in the design. Cut a length of lead slightly longer than you need and, working from one side of the glass across to the other side, stick the lead down. Once you have leaded all the short lines, move on to the longer ones, sticking the lead down over the cut ends of the lead on the short lines. This will keep the joins as neat as possible.

3 The lead is soft and flexible and will bend around quite tight curves. Stick it down in short sections, keeping one finger on the area already stuck and using the other hand to keep the lead taut while you position it.

4 Any ends of lead protruding over the edges of the glass can be trimmed off with scissors.

5 When you have finished the leading, flatten and smooth it with the end of a plastic pen or a wooden peg. Don't use anything metal, as it will mark the lead. Rub the pen over the lead, pressing it down onto the glass, and concentrating on the joins.

6 When all the lead is firmly stuck down, doodle a little clear water-based paint straight from the bottle onto the clear glass between the lead lines to add some texture.

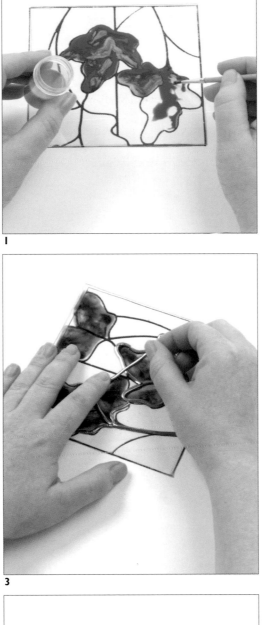

1

2

3

4

5

6

Outlining with paint

Outlining with paint allows you to create colourful designs that don't need further painting. Some paints are thick enough to be used from the bottle, while others must be thickened with a special agent. Wash out and re-use your old outlining bottles or you can make your own outlining bags.

MATERIALS
Square of greaseproof
   paper
Small pot
Water-based glass paint
Thickening agent
Stirring stick
Scissors
Release paper
Glass

1

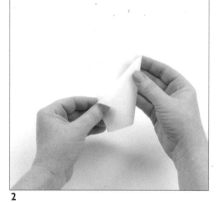

2

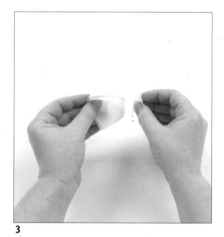

3

Making an outlining bag

1 Cut a square of greaseproof paper in half diagonally to make two triangles. Hold one triangle with the point towards you and the right-hand corner between your fingers.

2 Curl the right-hand corner over so that the tip touches the central point, making a cone.

3 Take the opposite corner right over the cone so that the tip touches the back of the central point, making a double-skinned cone.

4 Make sure that the cone is good and tight and then fold the central point into the cone twice.

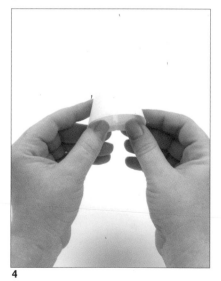

4

WHERE TO OUTLINE

You can use this outlining technique straight onto glass, either painted or plain, but it works better on a flat surface than on a curved one.

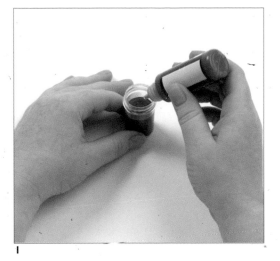

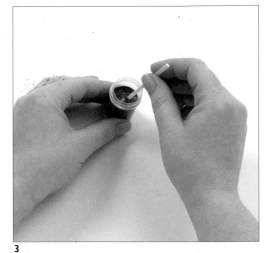

1

2

3

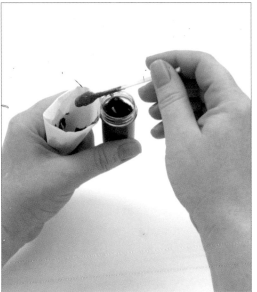

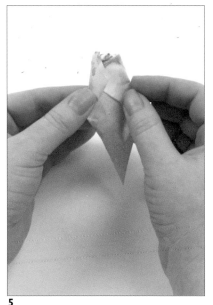

4

5

6

Thickening the paint

1 Squeeze some water-based paint into a small pot.

2 Add a drop or two of the thickening agent to the paint.

3 Mix the thickener slowly into the paint. A tea or coffee mixer is a good tool for this. If you mix too quickly you will introduce air bubbles into the paint and this will effect your ability to outline with it. If the paint is not thick enough to outline with, add more thickening agent, one drop at a time between stirrings.

Filling the outlining bag

4 Hold the outlining bag and paint pot in one hand and spoon the paint into the bag. Only half-fill the bag – if you overfill it the paint may spill out when you seal the bag.

5 Flatten the end of the outlining bag and fold in the outside flaps.

6 Tightly fold the end of the bag over a few times to hold the paint inside it.

7 Snip the very tip off the bag to make a hole to outline through. If it is too small you can always snip off a bit more.

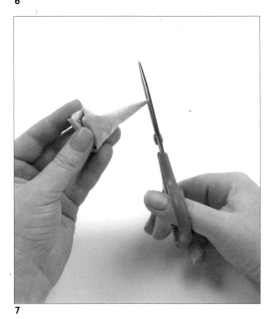

7

Outlining

1 Place a design under a piece of release paper and start outlining. You need to do each different-coloured section separately, allowing the first colour to dry before starting the second one. Outline the leaves in green paint.

2 Outline the centre of the flower in orange paint.

3 Outline the petals in yellow paint.

4 Outline the leaf veins in light green paint. Then let the whole design dry, either overnight or for a few hours in a warm place.

5 When the design is dry, it will just peel off the release paper. When you peel the design off you may stretch it a little, so just leave it upside down on the work surface for a few minutes and it will spring back into shape.

6 Lay the outlined design onto the glass and it will cling there by itself. If you want to fix it more permanently, spray the back with glue and stick it on.

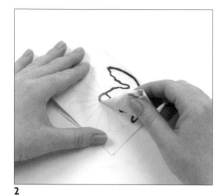

1

2

3

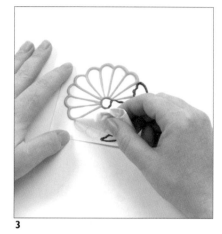

4

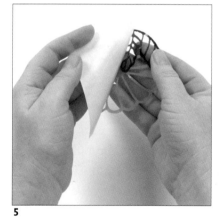

5

TAKING IT FURTHER

Coloured outlines laid on a sponged vase produce a vibrant, interesting piece of glass with minimum effort.

6

Painting water

A water effect is a simple one to do, but it looks very convincing. It makes a wonderful background for any seashore or marine project.

MATERIALS
Water-based glass paints in turquoise, deep aqua, royal blue and clear.
Paintbrush
Glass

1

2

3

4

1 Water the paints down to the consistency of single cream. Paint them onto the glass, using downward strokes rather than side-to-side strokes. Alternate colours and allow them to blend together as you paint.
2 Using a clean paintbrush, scatter some drops of water all over the wet paint.
3 Run the paintbrush down through the paint to spread the drops of water and blend the colours together further. Leave it to dry.
4 When the paint is dry, squeeze lines of clear paint straight from the bottle onto the surface. The lines should run from top to bottom, spaced randomly across the glass and curving and overlapping one another. Leave this to dry until the paint becomes clear.

Painting verdigris

Faux stone and metal effects are usually found on wood and walls, but there is no reason why you shouldn't use them on glass. With verdigris you need to work quickly, so that the colours blend and soften. You may have to experiment a little to get exactly the right colour balance, but remember that in this technique, less is more. You can build up colour, but you can't wipe off any excess.

MATERIALS
Water-based glass paints
  in amber, orange, aqua,
  white and turquoise
Gold outliner
Glass
Soft, smooth sponge
Paintbrush

1

2

3

4

1 Sponge a little amber and orange water-based paint onto the glass vase in random patches. Squeeze the paint onto a film-covered plate then dab the sponge into the paint and dab a little off onto the plate, so that you don't have too much on the sponge when you apply it to the glass. Use both colours together.

2 Using the same technique, sponge on aqua and white paints. Dip the sponge into both colours at once and randomly cover most of the glass, sponging over the edges of the amber and orange patches. Keep altering the angle of the sponge as you work to create dappled colour.

3 Sponge on a little turquoise paint, filling in any gaps and covering some of the previous colours. Do the same with gold outliner. You can also use the gold to highlight any detail in the glass. Leave to dry.

4 Roughly mix some aqua, turquoise and white paint; don't try to make one smooth colour, just swirl them together. Dilute the mixture to the consistency of single cream. Load a paintbrush with the diluted paint and drip it randomly down the sides of the vase. You can create as many drips as you wish, but start with a few and then add more.

Painting malachite

This is another faux effect that is rarely used on anything other than furniture or walls. However, glass paints capture the curious translucency and vibrant colour of malachite beautifully. A malachite window might look rather odd, but a malachite vase is beautiful.

MATERIALS
Water-based glass paints
  in kelly green and
  light green
Glass
Corrugated cardboard

1 Sponge the glass with light green paint and leave it to dry.
2 Squeeze the kelly green paint straight from the bottle onto the glass, applying it generously in sweeping lines from top to bottom of the glass. Fingerpaint the paint all over the glass, taking care not to miss any areas. Run your finger from top to bottom, smoothing the paint over the glass but not blending the colours any more than this.
3 Tear a jagged edge in a strip of corrugated card.
4 Using the jagged edge of the card as a comb, sweep it across the glass in smooth, uninterrupted strokes. As you comb, make small zig-zags with the card to create the natural ripples in malachite.

1

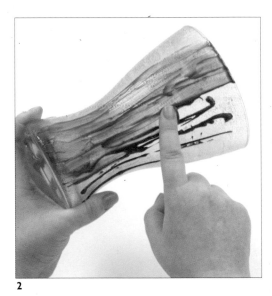

2

3

4

Sand painting

This is a wonderful technique that is also very versatile. You can use it to paint any flat surface, and if you want to use it on a curved surface, paint the design onto self-adhesive film and then cut it out and stick it on the glass.

This is a perfect answer for a window with an ugly view, as it completely blocks the view but, as the coat of sand is very thin, it still lets in light.

MATERIALS

Clear water-based
  glass paint
Glass or self-adhesive
  film
Sands in different
  colours
Paper
Paintbrush

1 Lay a sheet of paper over the worksurface to catch any excess sand. Place a piece of glass or film over the design and outline it in clear paint.

2 Before the paint dries, sprinkle your chosen sand or sands over the paint so that all the paint is covered. To sprinkle the sand, take a small rectangle of paper and fold it in half. Then fold one end over to seal it. This makes a simple paper scoop that you can fill with sand. If you tap the end it helps to guide your sprinkling.

3 Pick up the glass and tip all the excess sand off – a few taps on the back helps. Lay the glass aside to dry for about ten minutes. Tip the excess sand on the sheet of paper back into its pot.

4 Paint a few sections of the design at a time with clear paint. Paint right up to the outline, but not over it.

5 Sprinkle sand onto the painted areas. You can create graduated colours by sprinkling different coloured sands onto the wet paint. Either tip off the excess sand as you go and return it to its pot, or let the colours mix and make a new pot; you can get some great new colours this way.

6 Continue to paint the design section by section. On larger areas, use a thicker paintbrush to apply the clear paint so that you get an even coat. If you do miss a bit and the sand doesn't stick, wait until it is dry and then add a little more paint and fill in the gap with sand.

1

2

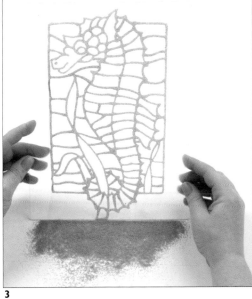

3

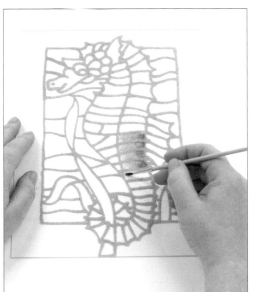

4

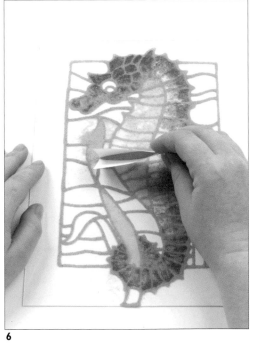

5

6

SUCCESSFUL SANDING

Work on a large sheet of white paper which has been folded in half, then opened out and laid flat. This will give you a natural crease, so any sand that falls onto the paper can be easily returned to the pot by picking up the paper and pouring it back.

If any of the outline smudges or wavers when you sand it, it is quite easy to just nudge it back into shape with the handle of a paintbrush before the paint dries. Once you have finished sanding your design, you can add more decoration. Simply outline decorative details in clear paint over the top of a dry sanded area, sprinkle a different coloured sand onto them and tip off the excess. You can add as much or as little extra detail as you wish, but the area you are adding to must be dry before you start.

Folk-art painting

This is a craft in itself and those of you who already practice it will find it simple to transfer your techniques to glass. For those who have never tried this before, here is a simple way to create the folk-art look on glass.

We have used a fine artist's brush throughout, but as you develop your skills in this type of painting, try experimenting with different brushes to create different strokes and effects.

MATERIALS
Water-based glass paints
Fine paintbrush
Glass

1

1 Squeeze a blob of red paint straight from the bottle onto a film-covered plate. Load the paintbrush with paint and make a simple heart-shaped petal with two brush strokes, so that the point of the heart faces towards you.

2

2 Add two more heart shapes in a row, each overlapping another.

3 Paint another two hearts just below the first three to make a simple flower head. Leave this to dry.

4 Load your paintbrush with some kelly green and light green paint and with two strokes swish the paint upwards to form a leaf shape. Paint another leaf on the other side of the flower head.

5 Add three more leaves, swishing them down from the flower head.

6 Using just the tip of the paintbrush and purple paint, paint three fine lines for stamens, rising up from the centre of the petals.

7 Add some dots of purple paint to the ends of the stamens and the centre of the flower.

8 Paint a random sprinkling of dot flowers. Make five small dots in a circle with blue paint and add a gold dot for the centre.

TAKING IT FURTHER

Practice making flowers of a piece of glass or acetate and then create a blooming vase. Paint the main flower around the glass several times and fill in the gaps with graceful leaves and a sprinkling of tiny, colourful dot flowers.

3

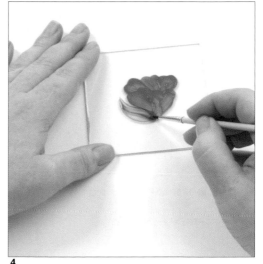

4

5

6

7

8

Granules and cookie cutters

Plastic glass painting granules and glass gravel bead granules can be obtained in various sizes and colours, and just by adding water-based paint to them they can be made into many things. Glass granules need to be left longer to dry out and harden up than plastic granules. If you try to take them out of the cutter too soon they may fall apart, so be patient.

MATERIALS
Cookie cutter
Margarine
Flat paintbrush
Plastic bowl
Granules
Water-based glass paint
Spoon
Release paper
Wire

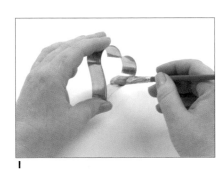

1

2

1 Whether you use a metal or a plastic cutter, you must grease it thoroughly to stop the paint and the granules sticking to it. Ordinary margarine makes an ideal and inexpensive grease. Just paint it onto the inside of the cutter with a flat paintbrush.

2 Pour some granules into an old plastic bowl.

3 Squeeze some paint straight out of the bottle into the bowl. A little goes a long way, so just squeeze in a small amount to start with, you can always add more.

3

4 Use an old spoon to mix the granules and paint together. The mixture should be quite stiff; if it is too runny, add some more granules. If the paint does not coat all the granules, add some more paint. If you make more of the mixture than you need, put the excess into a plastic bag, seal it and the mixture will keep until you need it again.

4

5 Place the greased cutter on a sheet of release paper or glass and spoon the granules into it. If you want a thin shape, then you can make it in one layer. If you want a thick shape, like the one we are making here, you will have to make it in two layers, so only half-fill the cutter with the granules.

5

6

6 Pat down the granules with the back of the spoon.

7 To make a hanger for the shape, bend a piece of wire in half to make a loop with the free ends crossed over one another.

7

8

8 Lay the free ends of the wire on the layer of granules so that the loop protrudes above the rim of the cutter.

9 When the first layer of granules is dry, you can spoon the second layer over the top of it. Make sure that the wire loop remains above the level of the granules.

9

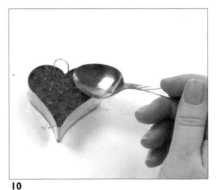

10

10 Pat the top of the granules down with the back of the spoon to make it as flat and smooth as possible. Leave it to dry overnight.

11 When dry, slide the cutter off the release paper and check that the bottom is also dry. If it isn't, leave the cutter upside down to allow the granules to dry completely.

When the granules are dry just push the shape out of the cutter. If it is stiff, stand it in some warm water for a few seconds and it will slide out easily. Wash the shape in soapy water to remove any traces of grease and hang it up by the wire loop.

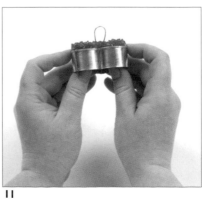

11

Granules and moulds

Plastic granules work brilliantly in moulds. Choose moulds that are simple, strong shapes – you won't get good results from detailed moulds as the granules won't go into all the nooks and crannies. You can get lots of moulds for free. Next time you unpack your shopping, just see how many products come in plastic shapes. Even yogurt pots and tubs can be used (save the lids to make stencils from).

MATERIALS

Mould	Spoon
Margarine	Sandpaper
Flat paintbrush	Ribbon
Plastic bowl	PVA craft glue
Granules	Silicone glue
Water-based glass paint	Gold outliner

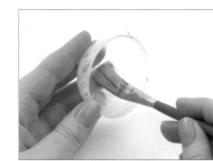

2

3

4

5

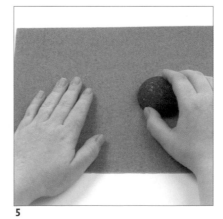

1

1 Grease the mould with margarine, painting it on with a paintbrush. Make sure you cover the whole surface as if any of the granules stick, the shape will be damaged. Remember that a mould only makes half a shape, so for a whole one you need two moulds. We are making a sphere.

2 Follow the technique used to mix the granules for the cookie cutters (see page 94), then spoon them into the mould.

3 To make a hollow sphere, use the back of a spoon to ease the layer of granules up the sides of the moulds. Make the top edges as flat as possible. Leave to dry overnight.

4 Tap the half-sphere out of the mould. If it sticks, just dip it into warm water for a few seconds and it will drop out. Wash off any grease and dry the half-sphere.

5 If the edges are a bit rough, place the half-sphere edge-down onto some coarse sandpaper and sand them smoother.

6

7

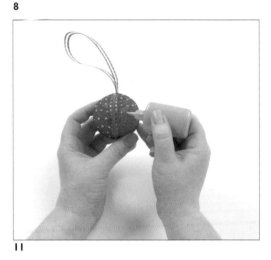

8

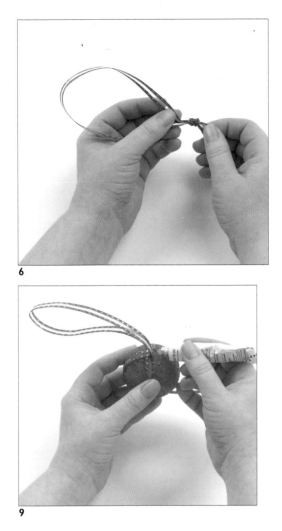

9

10

11

6 To turn the sphere into a hanging bauble, first knot the ends of a length of ribbon together.

7 Squeeze some craft or silicone glue around the edge of one half-sphere. Place the ribbon so that the knot is on the inside of the half-sphere.

8 Press the two half-spheres together to make a whole sphere. Put a strip of masking tape around the sphere to hold it together while the glue dries.

9 For a neat finish, cut two lengths of ribbon to the same size as the circumference of the sphere. Squeeze a blob of silicone glue onto the sphere on the join, next to the hanging ribbon.

10 Wind the ribbon around the sphere, covering the join, and glue the other end down. You may find

that you need another blob of glue at the bottom of the sphere to hold the ribbon in place. Glue the other length around the sphere at right angles to the first length.

11 Make tiny gold spots all over the bauble by squeezing on dots of outliner straight from the bottle.

TAKING IT FURTHER
This Christmas tree was made with a chocolate mould; the mould was made up of separate sections that stacked together to make a tree. We glued the sections together with silicone glue and then decorated the tree with glued-on glass nuggets.

Transferring photographs

These techniques are so easy that if you want anything easier we might as well come and do the glass painting for you. We have enlisted the help of technology for this one – you will need a computer scanner, an ink jet printer and some photographic paper.

MATERIALS
Photograph printed on
  photographic paper
Clear water-based glass
  paint
Paintbrush
Water
Spray glue
Glass

1

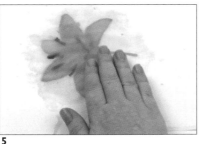

2

3

4

5

6

7

The outlining method

1 Scan the image you want to use and print it onto photographic paper, we used Kodak. We tried printing the design onto ordinary paper, but it just did not work.

2 While the ink is still damp, outline around all the sections of the picture with clear paint and let it dry a little. Then start filling in the sections with the paint, working on alternate sections.

3 When the first sections have dried a little, fill in the rest.

4 Let the whole design dry overnight. The paint will be white at first, but will dry clear.

5 When dry, turn the paper over and wet the back by dipping your fingers into water and then patting it onto the back of the paper. Let the water soak in.

6 The paint will peel off the paper quite easily. If it sticks, wet the paper a bit more. The ink in the picture will have been absorbed into the paint, though the colours will be paler than those on the original picture.

7 The paint will not be tacky, so you will have to spray some glue on the back of it to stick it to glass.

The fingerpainting method

If you don't like outlining, there is an even easier way of transferring a photograph onto paint.

1 Print the picture onto the photographic paper.

2 Squeeze a thick coat of clear paint onto the picture and fingerpaint it to cover the whole image. Leave to dry.

3 When the paint is completely dry, wet the paper on the back and peel the paint off the front, as before. Use scissors to straighten the ragged edges of the paint.

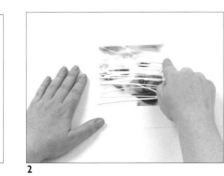
1

2

3

3-D pictures

You can add a 3-D effect to any of your craft and glass painting projects just by outlining a design with clear paint and filling in with more clear paint. However, you must choose an image that will not bleed colour into the paint, such as a postcard or greetings card.

MATERIALS

Image
Clear water-based glass
   paint

1 With some clear paint, outline the main sections of the design. Leave it to dry. Use the paint straight out of the bottle or an outlining bag.

2 Fill in the sections, letting each section dry before filling in the adjacent ones. When it is completely dry, paint on another layer in any areas you want to stand out further. The end result will be a shiny, raised image.

1

2

Embossing metal foil

Metal looks great painted with glass paints, as they give the shiny metal a jewel-like quality. You can buy metal foil in various finishes and with a self-adhesive backing – perfect for decorating glass. You can buy specialist embossing tools, but we find that a ballpoint pen works very well. You will find that the embossing process damages the paper template, so if you are repeating the design, photocopy it a few times, but remember to keep the original safe and don't use it.

MATERIALS

Self-adhesive metal foil
Paper template
Masking tape
Newspaper
Ballpoint pen
Scissors
Bradawl
Glass

1 Ensure that your paper template will fit onto the metal sheet.

2 Tape the template to the back of the metal. Remember that the design will come out in reverse on the front of the metal, so if you want the design the right way round, you will have to reverse the image.

3 Lay the metal on a pad of newspaper; this will protect your worksurface and provide a soft base on which to emboss the metal.

4 Trace over the design, applying pressure so that the lines are transferred through the paper onto the metal foil. Do a small section and then turn it over to check that you are pressing firmly enough and that the lines are coming through.

5 When you have embossed the design, cut it out roughly so that you have a smaller piece of metal to work with.

6 Place the metal back on the paper face upwards and, using a bradawl, punch holes through the metal, emphasizing the lines of the design. If you don't have a bradawl, the point of a compass will work just as well.

7 Cut out the design carefully using sharp scissors. Cut as close as possible to the embossed outside line, but don't cut over it.

8 Peel off the backing sheet, trying not to get your fingers on the adhesive side as this can make it less sticky.

9 Stick the metal onto either plain or painted glass. Rub it down gently to ensure that it is firmly stuck. You can embellish the glass further with lead strip (see page 82).

1

2

3

4

5

6

7

8

9

TAKING IT FURTHER

This lizard was made in exactly the same way as the silver ones, but the metal foil was fingerpainted with a thin coat of water-based glass paint before it was embossed.

Etching

This is a quick and easy etching technique that gives a sophisticated, contemporary result. It can be used to decorate any surface and the decorated item can be washed in the dishwasher quite happily. Although the etching fluid is very mild, you must always read and follow all safety instructions when using it, or any other etching medium. Wear gloves and goggles and mop up any spills quickly. This is definitely not a technique for children, in fact it is safest to keep them out of the room when you are etching.

MATERIALS
Safety equipment
Plastic container
Etching fluid
Glass
Glass nuggets
Silicone glue
Masking tape

STRAIGHT LINES

Check that the worksurface is completely flat before you start etching; use a spirit level to be sure. If the table is not level, the etched line on the glass will be crooked. Having said this, you might want to experiment with slanting lines, but be careful tipping the container of etching fluid and make sure that it is always safely supported.

1 Find a plastic container that will hold the glass – something a little bigger than the glass itself is ideal. Slowly pour the etching fluid into it without splashing. Pour in enough to etch the bottom third of the glass.

2 Place the glass carefully into the etching liquid. Put something, such as a book, on top to hold it down if you think it will float.

3 Check the instructions on the etching fluid bottle and after the required time, lift out the glass and wash off etching residue under running water, then dry the glass thoroughly.

4 Turn the glass the other way up and put it back into the etching fluid. Once again, use a book to weight it down if necessary. After the required time, remove the glass and wash and dry it, as before.

1

2

3

4

TAKING IT FURTHER

1

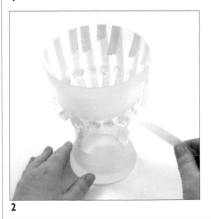

2

You can decorate etched glass further by attaching glass decorations, in this case, rough glass nuggets.

1 Squeeze a blob of silicone glue onto a flat side of a nugget and stick it onto the glass.

While the glue is drying, secure the nugget with a strip of masking tape. Repeat the sticking and taping process until you have stuck on as many nuggets as you want.

2 When the glue is dry, remove the masking tape.

Colour and sand painting

We have turned this project into a picture, but you could easily use it in a window to block out an unattractive view, or as a panel in a cupboard door, though you would have to protect it with another sheet of plain glass.

MATERIALS
Piece of extra thick film
Masking tape
Water-based glass paints
  in blue, light green,
  yellow, aqua, turquoise,
  kelly green, clear and
  purple.
Paintbrush
Sands in rose, purple,
  blue, green, yellow,
  white, natural, and
  aqua green.
Square picture frame
  with mount to fit

TECHNIQUES
Outlining with paint, see page 84
Sand painting, see page 90

1 Because this is a picture it is best to work on extra thick film to help keep the weight down.
Tape the design to the back of the extra thick film.

2 Either from an outlining bottle or an outlining bag, start outlining the design in your chosen colours. Here we have started with pink.

3 Start building up the paint outline changing the colours as you work to suit the design.

1

2

3

4 You can use as many different colours as you wish to complete the design. A combination of multi-coloured outlines and sands will produce a vibrant image. For a more restrained picture, limit your palette to two or three colours.

5 When you have outlined the whole design in paint, you must let it dry overnight.

6 When the outline is dry, paint one or two sections of the design at a time with clear paint. Paint right up to the coloured outline, but not onto it. Sprinkle sand on the paint, then tip off the excess. Graduate the colours in some areas by sprinkling one colour onto half of the wet paint and a second, toning colour onto the other half.

7 Build up the picture section by section, blending the sand colours as you work.

8 Once a section is dry you can add dots to it by dropping blobs of paint onto the sand and then sprinkling them with more sand in a contrasting colour. This will only work if the sand underneath is completely dry; if it is still wet the contrasting sand will stick to it.

9 Once you have finished the main picture, you can start filling in the background in the same way.

4

5

6

7

8

9

10 Once you have finished the picture, you can start adding detail if you wish. Outline shapes – in this instance, feathers – in clear paint over a sanded area.

11 Sprinkle sand over the outlined detail. You can continue to build up detail and colour to create a rich, complex design. When you have finished painting, leave it to dry and then give the whole picture a light coat of fixative.

10

11

Antiqued urn

A modern glass urn has been

painted and decorated for an

instant antique effect.

MATERIALS
Glass urn
Water-based glass paints
Sponge
Paintbrush
Self-adhesive metal foil
Newspaper
Ballpoint pen
Bradawl
3mm (⅛in) self-adhesive
  lead

TECHNIQUES
Painting verdigris, see page 88
Embossing metal foil, see page 100
Outlining with self-adhesive lead,
  see page 82

1 Paint the whole urn using the verdigris paint technique.

2 Add the trickles of watered-down paint to complete the effect. Leave the urn to dry.

3 Emboss and cut out enough bunches of grapes and vine leaves to decorate your glass.

4 Add detail to the vine leaves by piercing holes with the bradawl to represent veins.

5 Peel the backing off each embossed motif in turn and stick it to the painted urn.

6 Where the metal lies over a tight curve on the urn, you will have to press and manipulate it with your fingers to make it lie flat.

7 Peel the backing off a short section of a length of lead and, starting at the neck, wind it around the urn.

8 Continue wrapping the lead around, working your way down the urn. When you reach the base, cut off any excess lead and press it all firmly to the glass with your fingers.

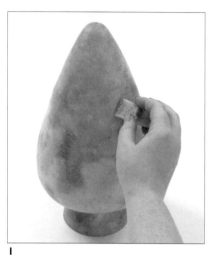

1

2

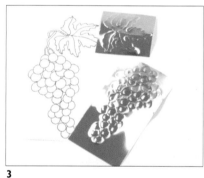

3

4

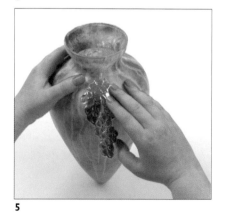

5

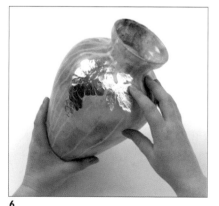

6

7

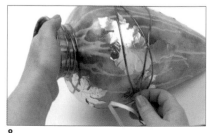

8

Folk-art tray

This is an interesting variation on the folk-art technique as it involves painting in reverse. As you are working on the back of the film, you have to paint all the highlights first and then the background colours. This project has been painted on pieces of extra thick film cut to fit the tray, which makes it easier to manage, but you could paint it on one sheet of film or glass.

MATERIALS

Tray
Pieces of extra thick film
    cut to fit the tray
Gingham rubber stamp
Water-based glass paints
    in turquoise, royal
    blue, white, yellow,
    light green, kelly green,
    gold, orange, red,
    brown and amber.
Flat and fine
    paintbrushes
6mm (¼in) wide brass
    self-adhesive lead

TECHNIQUES

Stamping an outline, see page 12
Folk-art painting, see page 92
Outlining with self-adhesive lead,
    see page 82

1 Decorate the side panels by stamping them. Turn the gingham stamp on its back and paint the face with turquoise paint. Use a flat paintbrush and apply the paint quite thickly.

2 Lay a side strip on the stamp, pressing it down and then lifting it off cleanly. Re-paint the stamp and then line the pattern up and repeat the process until you have stamped the whole strip. Stamp the remaining side trips in the same way.

3 Before you start the folk-art painting, photocopy your design and tape the relevant pieces to the relevant bits of film. We have used a large central panel, four small corner panels and four narrow side panels. Paint the dot flowers onto the corner panels. Leave to dry.

4 Paint the light green stems and leaves on the flowers and the yellow streaks on the petals. Leave to dry.

5 Paint over the yellow streaks with white petals. Leave to dry.

1

2

3

4

5

6 When you turn the corner piece over, the large flower is emerging from the dot flowers.

7 Lastly, add kelly green to the leaves and stems and base of the petals.

8 On the large piece of film, start by painting in the dot flowers and the stamens of the big flowers. As we wanted so many of these we made a separate template for the dots only.

9 Build up the dots: small flowers are blue with gold dot centres. Poppies have brown stamens with orange highlights. White flowers have amber, orange and yellow stamens.

10 Change to the main template and add highlights. Blue flowers have white highlights and ears of corn have brown and amber highlights.

11 Here is the panel with all the dots and highlights painted on. Leave this to dry.

12 Next, start painting in the flowers. Water down the paint a little so that it flows easily and start with the foreground flowers.

13 The poppies are red, the daisies white and the cornflowers blue. The ears of corn are painted in yellow and brown. The leaves are painted in different, blended shades of green.

14 If you are worried about how the piece is progressing, you can leave it to dry and turn it over to have a look. Keep painting until you are happy with the image. Leave to dry.

6

7

8

9

10

11

12

13

14

15 When all the pieces are completely dry, turn them upside down and arrange them on the tray. The pieces of film should fit neatly together. Notice that we have painted the corner panels as mirror images to create a symmetrical border for the main panel.

16 Cut four strips of lead the width of the tray and four the length of it. One at a time, peel the paper backing off a width strip and lay it down over the joins in the film and along the edges.

17 Use a craft knife to trim off any excess lead.

18 Press down the lead with the handle of a paintbrush or the end of a ballpoint pen. Finally, lead the lengthways joins and edges.

15

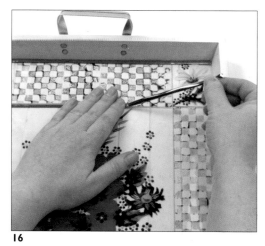
16

17

18

Decorated egg

You can really have fun with this project, decorating the egg with whatever you can lay your hands on. Rummage through old jewellry boxes for beads and baubles; bits of ribbon, trimmings and braid will also come in handy.

We used an egg mould for making chocolate eggs at Easter and plastic granules to fill it.

TECHNIQUES
Granules and moulds, see page 96
Attaching glass decorations, see page 25

I Grease the plastic egg mould. Mix your granules with the gold paint and spoon them into the mould, pressing the granules up to the top of the mould form a shell as the egg needs to have a hollow centre or it will never dry. Let the egg dry, preferably overnight. You will need to make two halves of the egg.

2 When the granules are dry, the egg should tip out of the mould. If it sticks, just dip the outside of the mould into warm water and it will tip out. If the granules are slightly soft on the outside, leave them to dry out for a while longer.

MATERIALS
Plastic granules
Gold water-based glass
  paint
Plastic egg mould
Grease
Silicone glue
Masking tape
Tea spoon
Braid
Gold fringe
Green and red glass
  hearts
Pearls
Glass jewels
Cord
Gold stars

I

2

3

4

5

6

7

8

9

3 If the edges of the mould are a bit rough, smooth them with some sandpaper. Squeeze some silicone glue all around the edge of one half-egg and stick the two halves together. A strip of masking tape around the middle will hold it together while it is drying.

When the two halves are stuck together, run some silicone glue right around the join. Starting at the bottom of the egg, stick the braid to the glue.

4 Continue all around the join in the egg. Then stick on another strip of braid to divide the egg into quarters. Finally, stick another strip of braid

around the middle of the egg: make sure that this strip is level as it will act as a guide for all the rest of the decoration.

5 Stand the egg in a cup, this makes it easier to decorate.

Now you can start to embellish the egg. Use silicone glue, which it thick and tacky enough to hold the decorations in place while they dry. Stick a strip of gold fringing around the egg and four green glass hearts around the top.

6 Stick a row of red glass hearts around the middle of the egg, just above the braid.

7 Glue pearl beads between and

above the hearts.

8 Flat-backed glass jewels are wonderful for egg-decorating – stick a row around the egg above the pearls.

9 When the top half of the egg is decorated, the glue has dried and everything is secure, turn the egg upside down. Coil braid around the lower half of the egg, gluing it down as you go. Leave a bare space right at the bottom of the egg so that it can sit on an egg stand. The final touch is a tiny crown formed from gold fringing and glued between the green hearts on top of the egg.

Good luck bowl

This is a sophisticated but simple project to make. Each nugget is etched with the Chinese symbol for good luck, so practice your outlining skills before you start. As with all etching projects, read the safety instructions on the bottle of etching fluid before you start and follow them carefully.

MATERIALS
2.5cm (1in) glass
   nuggets
Black outliner
Etching fluid
Craft knife
Glass bowl
Silicone glue

TECHNIQUES
Traditional outlining, see page 46
Etching, see page 102
Attaching glass decorations, see page 25

1

2

3

4

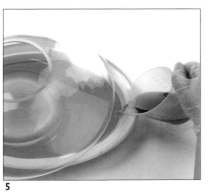

5

6

1 Reduce the Chinese good luck symbol on a photocopier to fit under the glass nuggets and outline the design. Leave them to dry in a warm oven or on a radiator, so that the outliner is completely dry and hard and doesn't lift off in the etching fluid.

2 Then when the outliner is dry, carefully place the nuggets into the etching fluid using a plastic spoon. Do not splash the fluid. Leave to etch for the recommended time.

3 When they are ready, carefully lift out the nuggets and wash them in clear water. Dry them and then, with a craft knife, peel away the outliner to reveal the clear design on the glass.

4 Though the nuggets are small, the symbol stands out clearly.

5 Stand the bowl in a plastic or ceramic container and carefully pour in the etching fluid around it. It is important that the container is standing on a level surface and that you do not splash the glass with the etching fluid as you pour. Leave the bowl for the recommended time and then remove it and wash and dry it.

6 Put a blob of silicone glue on the back of each nugget and stick them at equally spaced intervals around the rim of the bowl.

Motif library

In this section of the book you will find many of the specially designed

motifs used for both the techniques and projects in the previous chapters.

Outliner in sheets,
see page 13

Outliner on self-adhesive film,
see page 14

Texture from patterned surfaces,
see page 28

Star-burst candle lantern,
see page 40

Traditional outlining,
see page 46

Metallic paints,
see page 51

Oriental lacquer effect,
see page 52

Oriental lacquer effect,
see page 52

Metallic paints,
see page 51

Embedding beads,
see page 56

Embedding beads,
see page 56

Embedding beads,
see page 56

Colouring fabric,
see page 62

Beaded rainbow catcher,
see page 77

Oriental candle sconce,
see page 68

Outlining with self-adhesive lead,
see page 82

Outlining with paint,
see page 84

Embossing metal foil,
see page 100

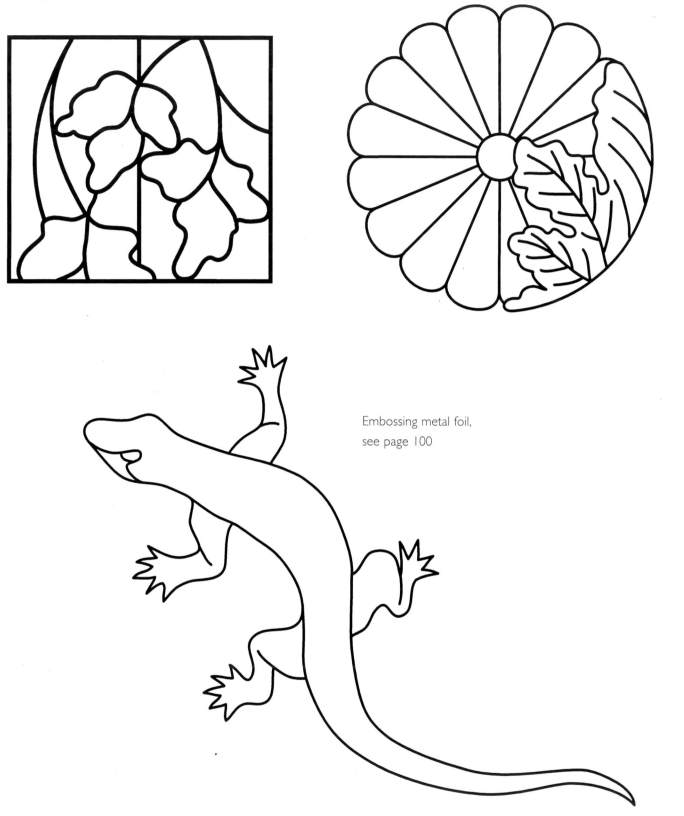

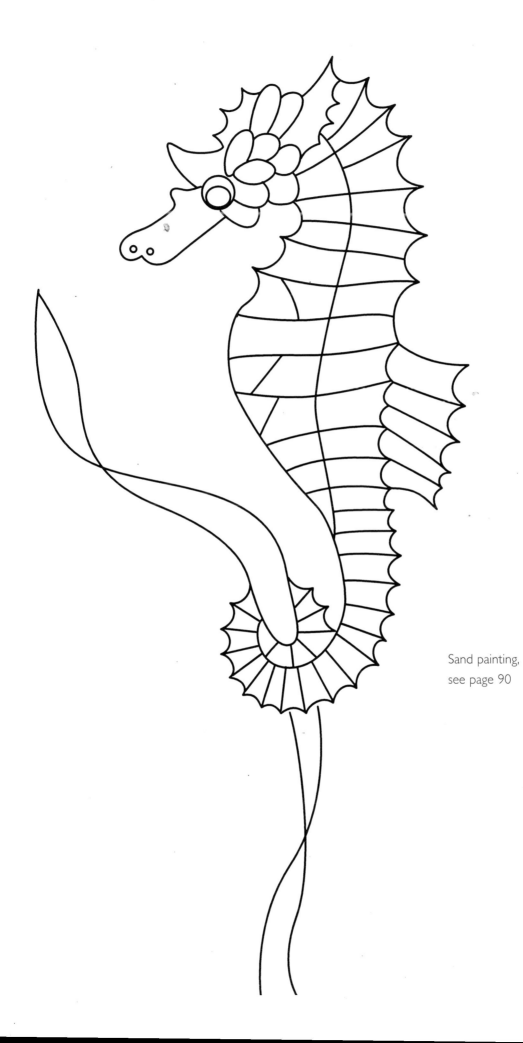

Sand painting,
see page 90

Colour and sand painting,
see page 104

Antiqued urn,
see page 108

Glossary

Outliner

Outliner comes in tubes or bottles of various colours, usually black, grey, gold and silver. The outlining gives the glass a leaded look, rather like a stained glass window, and also acts as a wall to separate your colours.

Outlining bag

This is a triangle of greaseproof or parchment paper formed into a cone and filled with the outliner. It can also be filled with glue or paint and is a really useful tool.

Rainbow Glass water-based paints

These child-safe water-based paints are concentrated so they can be watered down to the consistency that you need to work with. It is best not to water them down more than one part paint to one part water as if you add too much water they will dry with a frosted finish. These paints can also be mixed together to produce any colour you want. Mixing may introduce air bubbles, so leave the paint to stand until they have disappeared before you start working. If the paint is applied thinly it will dry in minutes. The thicker the paint, the longer it will take to dry, though you can use a hair dryer to speed up the drying time. Clean your paintbrush by washing it in water.

Thickening agent

This liquid agent will thicken the water-based paint so that you can use it to outline with. Add the thickening agent one drop at a time, stirring slowly until the required thickness is achieved.

Rainbow Glass solvent-based paints

These are the traditional paints used for glass painting. They appear only once in this book as they do take some time to dry. Always use them in a well-ventilated room. Do not shake the bottle as you will introduce air bubbles into the paint. Clean your paintbrush by squeezing the bristles between a piece of kitchen towel until there is no trace of the paint left, or you can use a good quality cellulose thinners.

Paintbrushes

A number 2 soft-bristled brush is ideal for most of the projects in this book, while a flat-ended, wide brush will cover larger areas smoothly.

Spray paints

There are various spray paints on the market giving many different effects. Always follow the manufacturer's instructions before using sprays.

Clear self-adhesive film

This film has a sheet of release film over the sticky side. Before you start you must check that you are painting on the side with the sticky back. Do this by peeling away one corner of the backing. If you find it difficult to peel away, stick a piece of sticky tape on either side of the corner and then pull them apart a little way. Remember you are only doing this to find out which is the sticky side of the film, you must not peel away the protective sheet at this stage or you will not be able to use the film.

You can outline and paint the film and when dry, cut out the design close to the outliner, remove the backing sheet exposing the sticky side and stick it directly onto your project.

Copy film

This self-adhesive glass painting film is good for many techniques: rubber stamping or embedding fabric for example. It can also, as its name suggests, be put through a photocopier so you can photocopy any design to use as an outline. Once dry, remove the backing sheet and stick the design to any smooth surface.

Cling film

You can outline onto this film, paint and cut out the design, then peel away the backing sheet and the film will cling to any smooth surface.

Thick film

This film is 500 microns thick, which makes it rigid but also bendable. It is perfect for making items like mobiles or cards as it can be cut easily with scissors or a craft knife.

Extra-thick film

This film is 1000 microns thick and is a good replacement for glass. It is a rigid film that keeps its shape when cut with sturdy scissors or a heavy-duty craft knife. For intricate designs, we find a hot knife is best cutting tool.

If you score a straight line in the film with a blunt tool, such as the tip of a flat-headed screwdriver, the film will bend along the line and not split or crack. Both the thick and the extra-thick films have a protective covering on either side that must be removed an hour or so before you want to work because peeling the covering away creates static electricity which will make your outliner jump when you try to use it.

Release paper

This paper is coated so that if you outline or paint onto it you will be able to peel away the outliner or paint once dry.

Self-adhesive lead

The self-adhesive lead we use is coated so that you don't get lead on your fingers. If you use un-coated lead, wear thin gloves when handling it. Do not smoke or handle food until you have washed your hands.

Keep the lead at room temperature so that it stays supple. If it is cold it will be harder to work with.

Lead can be bought in various colours, usually in antique lead, black, brass, platinum, and in assorted thicknesses.

Suppliers

UK

Rainbow Glass
85 Walkden Road
Worsley
Manchester M28 7BQ
Tel: 0161 790 3025
Website: www.rainbowglass.co.uk
Water-based and solvent-based glass paints, self-adhesive films, self-adhesive lead, etching cream.

LJ Gibbs & Partners Ltd
Mulberry House
Hewitts Road
Chelsfield, Nr Orpington
Kent BR6 7QS
Tel: 01959 533663
Email: info@ljgibbsandpartners.com
Website: www.ljgibbsandpartners.com
Hand-made papers